W9-BLJ-152

# FANTASTIC
# FLYING
# MACHINES

# FANTASTIC FLYING MACHINES

## MICHAEL J.H. TAYLOR

**JANE'S**

LONDON · NEW YORK · SYDNEY

Copyright © Michael J. H. Taylor 1981

First published in the United Kingdom in 1981 by
Jane's Publishing Company Limited
238 City Road, London EC1V 2PU

ISBN 0 7106 0125 5

Published in the United States of America in 1982 by
Jane's Publishing Incorporated
730 Fifth Avenue
New York
N.Y. 10019

ISBN 0 531 03737 1

All rights reserved. No part of this publication may be reproduced,
stored in a retrieval system, transmitted in any form or by any means
electrical, mechanical or photocopied, recorded or otherwise
without prior permission of the publisher.

Designed by Bernard Crossland Associates

Typeset in Great Britain by
D. P. Media Limited,
Hitchin, Hertfordshire

Printed in Italy by
Arnoldo Mondadori Editore, Verona

# CONTENTS

# 1. The Capricious Years

There is nothing new about flight in the air, or fantastic fliers. It must be remembered that the specialised and sophisticated flight capability of birds and insects has evolved during the trials and errors of some 65 million years. In some respects, man has done rather better within the timescale of only 177 years, if one accepts Sir George Cayley's model glider of 1804 as the world's first successful free-flying heavier-than-air craft. From that date enthusiastic pioneers, researchers, designers and engineers have created the entire gamut of civil, military and research aircraft which have flown – or failed to fly!

A close study of aviation and ornithological history will pinpoint many stepping stones which have led to the evolution of aircraft and birds which fly in our modern skies. Nature's self-selecting process of development, depending on the survival of the fittest, can often be traced by the absence in today's world of creatures which are known to have existed. Many of nature's more fantastic projects just withered and died.

In the case of aviation history we are rather more fortunate, for whilst there are many early projects about which we would like to have considerably more detail, the basic advances are clearly defined. Much of the experimentation and development that followed the first man-carrying, powered and sustained flight of a heavier-than-air craft, achieved by the Wright brothers in 1903, has been well documented. However, *Fantastic Flying Machines* does not set out to document the history of aviation, but instead draws attention to a small number of aircraft, all of unusual configuration or purpose, which have enriched man's knowledge of flight. No doubt some, especially those of years gone by, caused a 'chuckle' from the sidelines. While a few proved dead-ends technically, others were inspired, only their radically unusual appearances preventing series production. Later chapters include unusually-shaped but excellent production and homebuilt

**Maxim's biplane**

**Phillips *Multiplane* of 1904**

aircraft, including some of the most popular aircraft ever built.

Perhaps the most difficult task is to know where to begin, for the majority of 'pioneering' aircraft of the 'stick and string' decade preceding the outbreak of the Great War of 1914–18 were of curious form. Viewed from the '80s we accept the myriad of struts, wires and structural members as necessary given the technology of the day. So, by accepting the 'norm', however alien to modern thinking, it is possible to extract the unusual.

In the year following the Wright brothers' success in America, and a full ten years after Sir Hiram Maxim's 372 m² (4,000 sq ft) biplane lifted briefly from the ground, a Briton named Horatio Phillips constructed what can only be called a powered venetian blind. With twenty wings, each of only a few inches chord, it was tested but proved a failure. Not willing to bow to the more conventional biplane or triplane layout, he produced another Multiplane in 1907 of even stranger appearance. This time he adopted four blinds in tandem, each with more than forty narrow chord wings. The 22 hp engine drove a single tractor propeller. Undoubtedly to most people's astonishment, but not his, it 'hopped' for a distance of about 152 m (500 ft) and is often claimed as the first powered aeroplane to have flown in Great Britain. As a matter of history, the first 'officially recognised' flight in Britain was made in October 1908 by Samuel Franklin Cody in the Army Aeroplane No 1, covering nearly three times that distance.

By 1911 the English Channel had been conquered by Blériot, Alfred Leblanc had raised the speed record to nearly 110 km/h (68 mph) and

*Above:* Phillips 1907 *Multiplane*          *Below:* Dixon Nipper No 1    (*Flight International*)

**Edwards Rhomboidal**  *(Flight International)*

**Siemens-Schuckert Dr. I**  *(Imperial War Museum)*

**Caproni Triple Hydro-Triplane**

night flights had been achieved, but still there were those who rebelled against the proved configurations. Perhaps taking a lead from Alberto Santos-Dumont's 14*bis* of 1906, H.S. Dixon produced the Dixon Nipper. Without the pilot it looked fairly conventional – a tractor-engined monoplane with an all-moving tailplane. However, Dixon decided everyone else was wrong and sat facing the 'tail', which became a canard unit. The power plant likewise became a pusher, fitted with the appropriate two-blade propeller. Sufficient to say it was subsequently lost in an accident.

Another unorthodox aeroplane of 1911 was the Edwards Rhomboidal which, like the Nipper, featured in replica form in the outstanding film *Those Magnificent Men In Their Flying Machines* (Twentieth Century-Fox Productions Ltd).

The four war years from 1914 abounded with new concepts both practical and impractical. Designers were stretched to their limits attempting to comply with ever more demanding military requirements, with the result that many unconventional aircraft reached prototype stage. Inevitably, most were abandoned before or soon after their first flights. One such aircraft was the German Siemens-Schuckert Dr.I, a 'push and pull' triplane with outriggers supporting the tail unit, designed as a fighter following the success of the British Sopwith Triplane on the Western Front from early 1917. Like the original Fokker Dr. triplane which featured cantilever wings, the innovations introduced by Siemens-Schuckert were incorporated to improve upon the British fighter. Despite a more conventional version of the Fokker aircraft entering service from August 1917, development of the Siemens-Schuckert continued. Undoubtedly boosted by the grounding of the Fokker from October to December, after several had crashed during operations through suspected failure of the wing structure, it was rolled out for its first flight in November, during which it crashed. So ended the career of the Siemens-Schuckert Dr.I, while the Fokker Dr.I went on to become one of the legendary fighters of the war, best remembered as the mount of the 'Red Baron', Manfred von Richthofen.

Early in the war Italy had realised the potentialities of strategic bombing with giant aircraft, and from August 1915 waged the first ever sus-

## Dornier Do X

tained operation against Austro-Hungary with Caproni Ca 2s flying across the Alps. For the rest of the war Caproni specialised in heavy bombers, but with the coming of peace the company naturally applied itself to large commercial aircraft. During 1920 Caproni busied itself in the production of an enormous flying-boat with accommodation for 100 passengers. Even this giant, known officially as the Triple Hydro-Triplane but colloquially as the 'Capronissimo', was intended only as an outsized model from which to obtain data for a much larger transatlantic seaplane.

Powered by eight 400 hp Liberty engines, each engine with its own engineer, the Triple Hydro-Triplane had three sets of triplane wings equally spaced along the length of the hull. The only elevators consisted of small vanes between the hull and the wing-floats and were intended to assist the hull in leaving the water. The flying-boat made its first taxiing trials on Lake Maggiore towards the end of February 1921, and on 2 March managed a flight of about 1.6 km (1 mile)

in a straight line. However, two days later a further flight was attempted, during which contemporary reports state that it proved unstable and uncontrollable longitudinally, resulting in a bad landing which caused considerable damage.

As a nation Italy continued to develop flying-boats during the 1920s and 1930s, having considerable success with much smaller aircraft built for civil and military use. It also received two examples of the German Dornier Do X during this period, named *Umberto Maddalena* and *Alessandro Guidoni*.

First flown on 25 July 1929, having been constructed at Altenrhein in Switzerland, the Do X was by far the largest aeroplane in the world. Powered by twelve 525 hp Siemens-built Bristol Jupiter engines mounted in tandem pairs above the 48 m (157 ft 5 in) monoplane wing, it had been designed to carry up to 150 passengers. The Jupiter engines were subsequently exchanged for Curtiss Conquerors. On 21 October 1929 the first Do X for German use took off with a full load of passengers and a crew of ten, plus an incredible nine stowaways.

Able to cruise at 190 km/h (118 mph) and with a service ceiling of just 500 m (1,640 ft), it left Friedrichshafen on 2 November 1930 for a flight in stages to New York, which it reached on 27 August 1931 after an eventful crossing which included damage to the wing and hull. As a commercial aircraft it proved totally impractical; the two sister 'boats built for an Italian airline company were taken over by the military.

In contrast to the Do X the contemporary Junkers G 38 was an outstanding success, the second aircraft continuing to operate with Deutsche Luft Hansa (after the first had crashed in 1936) until the war, when it was destroyed during an RAF raid. First flown on 6 November 1929, the G 38 was a most remarkable airliner with huge monoplane wings of 44.0 m (144 ft 4 in) span. Power was eventually provided by four 750 hp Junkers Jumo 204 engines mounted in the leading-edges of the wings, each driving a large propeller. Cruising speed was 208 km/h (129 mph). One of the most interesting features was its passenger accommodation, with seating for three passengers in each of two cabins in the wing roots, two

**Junkers G 38**

**Granville brothers' Gee Bee Super-Sportster**

passengers in the extreme fuselage nose and a further 26 in the main cabin. The second G 38 even had a smokers' cabin in the tail. Interestingly the Japanese manufacturer Mitsubishi produced in secrecy a military version of the G 38 as the Ki-20, followed by five more by 1934. Intended as a strategic bomber with the capability of reaching targets in the Philippines, it was not well received and never saw action.

Across the Atlantic in the USA the Granville brothers were stunning crowds at National Air Races with a series of Gee Bee aircraft; sleek, fast and highly competitive machines built to the principle of the maximum sized engine in the minimum airframe. In total seven Gee Bees were produced, all of which eventually had accidents, some pilots being killed. By far the best remembered is the Super-Sportster, in which the daring pilot sat in a small enclosed cockpit just ahead of

the tailplane. All engine controls were grouped together for use by the pilot's left hand, the throttle control being strong enough to be used as a hand hold for rough weather flying.

Flying the Super-Sportster with an 800 hp Pratt & Whitney Wasp engine, James Doolittle (famed as the first man to fly across the United States in a single day in 1924; later to lead sixteen North American B-25 Mitchell bombers in the first raid on the Japanese mainland during World War II, flying from the aircraft carrier USS *Hornet* and attacking Tokyo) won the 1932 Thompson Trophy Race at an average speed of 406.5 km/h (252.6 mph). In September he flew the same aircraft to establish a new world landplane speed record of 476.74 km/h (296.29 mph). For the 1933 National Air Races the Super-Sportster was provided with a 900 hp Pratt & Whitney Hornet supercharged engine. While competing in the

Bendix Trophy Race the aircraft unfortunately met with an accident and its owner/pilot, Russell Boardman, was killed.

Throughout the 1930s the British Westland company experimented with tailless aircraft as versions of the Pterodactyl, originated in the 1920s by Captain G.T.R. Hill and later known as Westland-Hill types. Captain Hill's intention was to produce an aeroplane immune from the dangers attendant upon stalling in a conventional machine. Quoting from the 1927 edition of *Jane's All the World's Aircraft*: 'The essential feature of Capt Hill's design is the use of a wing section having a stationary centre of pressure throughout the normal range. The result of using such a wing is that the horizontal control and stabilizing surfaces are not subject to a trimming load which changes with the angle of attack of the wings, and can consequently be arranged so that they lie very nearly along the relative wind direction, whatever angle the wings proper may be at. Thus, even when the Hill type is stalled, the horizontal control surfaces are capable of producing large controlling forces and the type can be manoeuvred in the normal way under conditions in which the normal aeroplane is uncontrollable.'

Originally tested as a glider, the Pterodactyl was subsequently modified to include a 32 hp Bristol Cherub engine and pusher propeller and a simple undercarriage. In this form it was flown in the spring of 1926, proving to have amazing controllability under all conditions and good all-round performance. Steering was by means of two movable vertical rudders fitted below the swept wings. Carried from the ends of the fixed wings were a pair of pivoted surfaces known as 'controllers', which could be used as elevators or ailerons. In powered form the Pterodactyl was known as the Mark IA, and when it was taken over by the Air Ministry it was given the military serial J8067.

From the Mark IA was developed a more powerful two-seat version with an 80 hp Armstrong Siddeley Genet engine. This had a novel undercarriage arrangement, comprising tandem main wheels under the short fuselage and outriggers under the wings to balance the aircraft. The vertical rudders of the Mark IA were removed, but the later Mark IV reintroduced these on the wingtips. However, the Mark IV was very different from those preceding it. Most noticeable was that it appeared as a cabin monoplane with accommodation for a pilot and two passengers. The undercarriage layout of the two-seater was retained, but power was provided by a 120 hp de Havilland Gipsy III inverted engine mounted as a pusher. For visual effect, a 'paint job' depicted for a time the winged reptile from which it derived its name, complete with open mouth and bared teeth.

Undoubtedly the most interesting version of the Pterodactyl was the Mark V, built by Westland

**Westland-Hill Pterodactyl Mark IV** *(Westland Aircraft)*

**Pterodactyl Mark V    *(Westland Aircraft)***

as a two-seat fighter. Powered by a tractor-mounted 600 hp Rolls-Royce Goshawk engine, it introduced a sesquiplane wing arrangement. Control was by balanced flaps on the swept upper wing, which acted as elevators or ailerons. Automatic wingtip slats were fitted. Pilot and rear-gunner were situated aft of the wings and had exceptional all-round vision, the gunner seated slightly lower in the tail of the short fuselage. Although the Pterodactyl Mark V never went into production and the concept was abandoned by Westland, other designs for tailless aircraft were produced in Britain and Germany shortly before and during World War II, and Northrop in the USA went much further once peace had again been restored (see The Flying Wings). Indeed, the German Gotha Go 147 observation aircraft of 1936–38 was very similar to the Pterodactyl. Despite its appearance, the Pterodactyl Mark V was built as a serious contender for production orders and was fully capable of aerobatics. Peculiar perhaps, unique in Britain certainly, but it was a measure of Westland's faith in the basic idea that it was willing to go against so many conventions with the Pterodactyl. The Mark IA is preserved today in the Science Museum.

During the same period Soviet Tupolev TB-1 and TB-3 heavy bombers were used in the famous 'Zveno' parasite experiments. The TB-1 carrying two Tupolev I-4 or Polikarpov I-5 biplane fighters above the wings, and with the four-engined TB-3 carrying three I-5s above and two I-16 fighters below, each bomber would take off and later air-launch the fighters as protection against simulated enemy attack. Interesting as these experiments were, Soviet parasite fighters were used only once or twice operationally, in about August 1941.

The 'pick-a-back' concept was, however, used both successfully and commercially in Britain as the revolutionary Short-Mayo Composite. Basically the Composite consisted of a very highly loaded seaplane named *Mercury* mounted on top of another comparatively lightly loaded aircraft to form a composite aircraft capable of taking-off easily and quickly under normal operating conditions. When the composite aircraft had climbed to a suitable height, *Mercury* was released from the strengthened 'Empire' class flying-boat *Maia* lower component. In this manner *Mercury* was capable of carrying a fuel load and cargo with which it would have been incapable of taking-off by itself. Thus transatlantic routes were within its range.

The Composite was built by Short Brothers at Rochester to an Air Ministry contract for experimental use by Imperial Airways. The specification required *Mercury* to have a range of approximately 5,630 km (3,500 miles) when carrying 453 kg (1,000 lb) of mail, which was

**Loading three I-5s on to a TB-3 during 'Zveno' parasite experiments** *(Tass)*

*Mercury* **leaves** *Maia*

sufficient for the direct North Atlantic crossing in continuous headwinds of 97 km/h (60 mph). *Mercury* and *Maia* were completed in late 1937 and, after tests with each aircraft individually, the first separation of the Composite was achieved on 6 February 1938. Having been handed over to Imperial Airways, the Composite took off from Foynes, Ireland, on 21 July and *Mercury* went on to fly non-stop to Montreal with mail and newspapers. After refuelling *Mercury* flew on to New York, completing the journey from Foynes in a flying time of 22 hours 31 minutes. The return journey was made in stages. During 6–8 October *Mercury* flew from Dundee in Scotland non-stop to the Orange River in South Africa, so exceeding the previous longest distance flown by a sea-going aircraft by 1,335 km (830 miles). Many other composite flights were made and the aircraft served the Southampton–Alexandria route right up to the outbreak of World War II. Interestingly, *Mercury* had a maximum speed of 341 km/h (212 mph), but averaged 225 km/h (140 mph) on its first Atlantic crossing, while the Composite flying as an eight-engined aircraft

had a normal cruising speed of 233 km/h (145 mph).

Many unorthodox aircraft appeared on the aviation scene just prior to or during World War II, some of the most interesting German types conceived out of desperation during the final years of the war. One example was the 'push and pull' Dornier Do 335 Pfeil fighter, which was nearly ready for operational deployment at the end of the war. Another was the Bachem Ba 349 Natter, produced as a near vertically-launched rocket-powered interceptor with an endurance of a few minutes only. Armament comprised either 24 or 33 rockets housed in the nose. The nose section of the aircraft was considered expendable, the remaining section and the pilot decending by parachute after the interception. The first launch of a Natter with a volunteer pilot was made on 28 February 1945, but ended in tragedy. However, subsequent tests proved more successful and eventually limited production was started. Only a few Natters were completed, ten of which were put on operational status in April to attack USAAF bombers on daylight raids. However, advancing

**Abandoned German aircraft include a damaged Dornier Do 335 Pfeil    (*US Air Force*)**

*Right:* **Bachem Ba 349 N**

**Blohm und Voss Bv 141**

Allied ground forces found the remains of these before a single mission had been flown.

Probably the strangest looking aircraft of any combatant nation to be used operationally was another German type, the Blohm und Voss Bv 141. Best remembered as a manufacturer of flying-boats, Blohm und Voss was formed from the earlier Hamburger Flugzeugbau company, which had originated the aircraft as the Ha 141 in 1937. The Bv 141 was a short-range reconnaissance and army co-operation aircraft, the asymmetric layout intended to allow the maximum field of vision with a single-engined type. The BMW radial engine was mounted in the nose of the offset fuselage and the crew of three were accommodated in a nacelle alongside and to starboard. The asymmetric braced tailplane extended on most models to the port side of the fin. In the event it was a change of policy that ended the production of the Bv 141 after only a small number had been completed, although a few became operational on the Eastern Front from late 1941.

Others too were capable of radical design. In 1939 Curtiss, having won a US Army fighter competition with its P-40 Warhawk, was busy also constructing a prototype Helldiver dive-bomber for the US Navy and working on its most unusual project to date, the XP-55 Ascender single-seat tail-first fighter. First flown at Scott Field, Illinois, on 13 July 1943, the Ascender was powered by a 1,275 hp Allison V-1710 engine mounted at the aft end of the fuselage and driving a three-blade pusher propeller. An air intake was positioned above the engine and a coolant radiator duct below, both being incorporated in rectangular vertical stabilising surfaces. Two 20 mm cannon and four 0.50 in machine-guns were positioned in the nose of the fuselage of the third prototype, which achieved a maximum speed of 627 km/h (390 mph).

In 1944 North American constructed the first prototype of its XP-82 escort fighter, designed to protect USAAF bombers on long-range missions in the Pacific theatre of war. Known as the Twin Mustang, it was exactly that: two P-51 Mustang

**Curtiss XP-55 Ascender**  *(US Air Force)*

**North American F-82 Twin Mustang**  *(US Air Force)*

**Chance Vought V-173**

fighters joined with a new constant-chord centre-wing and rectangular centre tailplane. Both engines and pilots' cockpits remained, the latter feature allowing the pilots to fly the aircraft in turn on a long mission. The fighter proved highly successful during tests and massive production was started. However, only a very small number of production P-82Bs had been built by the end of the war, and no more were constructed after November 1945. But in the following year the Twin Mustang was evaluated as a night fighter and another 250 were ordered as escort and night fighters. Interestingly, an F-82 (as the aircraft was subsequently redesignated) destroyed the first 'enemy' aircraft during the Korean War of the early 1950s.

The major prize for originality must, nevertheless, go to Chance Vought for its XF5U-1 programme, intended to produce a fighter with a wide speed range and one which could actually hover at low or zero speeds. The design was for an aircraft with a wing of roughly circular planform which constituted the main structure. The engines were buried in the wing, one on each side of the cockpit, driving four-blade propellers with articulated blades which could function in a similar way to a helicopter's rotor blades. Although built the XF5U-1 never flew, but a full-scale lower-powered version, the V-173, first flew on 23 November 1942.

# 2. Fantastic Fighters since 1945

World War II ended in August 1945 with the biggest man-made explosions the world had known. Two atomic bombs, innocently named *Little Boy* and *Fat Man*, put the Japanese cities of Hiroshima and Nagasaki in the history books for ever, whilst virtually wiping them from the face of the earth. The age of the nuclear deterrent was born.

Repercussions were many, not least of which was to ensure that the aircraft industries of all major powers avoided a re-enactment of the severe depression caused by cancelled contracts after World War I. Further, the advent of the jet fighter and bomber, exploited principally by Germany and Britain during World War II, forced the appropriation of huge sums of money for the replacement of piston-engined aircraft with higher performance jets.

Pulse-jets and rocket engines had really been the domain of Germany, although other countries, including Japan, had researched along similar lines. These engines had powered Germany's 'terror weapons' – the V-1 flying-bomb and V-2 ballistic missile – the latter engine type being used also in the diminutive Messerschmitt Me 163 Komet interceptor (and the Natter – see the first chapter), which had an endurance of just eight minutes with power on and claimed nine Allied aircraft destroyed in operations from August 1944 to early 1945. However, German wartime research had progressed far beyond the more generally known operational weapons.

Disregarding the array of successful and unsuccessful first generation missiles designed for air-to-air, air-to-surface, anti-tank, anti-aircraft and other purposes, German manufacturers had

**Messerschmitt P.1101** *(MBB)*

**Bell X-5**   (*Bell Helicopter Textron*)

**Convair Sea Dart**                                              *Right:* **Convair XFY-1 Pogo**   (*General Dynamics*)

**Saunders-Roe SR.A/1**

researched, and in some cases built prototypes of, many futuristic aircraft. Blohm und Voss, Junkers and Messerschmitt had designs for tailless swept-wing fighters, while Lippisch combined delta wings and a huge vertical tail containing the pilot's cockpit with ramjet power. Large delta wings with swept tips were featured in one of the Focke-Wulf bomber projects, while Messerschmitt's P.1101 prototype jet fighter, with wings which could be set at various angles of sweep for research purposes, formed subsequently the basis of Bell's X-5 aircraft (flown 1951). Similarly, many features of the Focke-Wulf Ta 183 appear to have been incorporated in several of the first Soviet jet fighter designs.

It was against such advanced projects attaining any degree of fruition that the Allies had waged much of its strategic bombing campaigns. Equally, advancing American, British,

French and Soviet forces seized as much documentation and as many items of hardware as they could find as the Third Reich collapsed.

Although much of the German wartime technology was analysed and digested, it was the future potential threat from high-speed, long-range bombers carrying incredible loads of conventional or atomic weapons, and the verbal war between nations, that forced fighter design quickly into new realms.

How safe was an airfield from enemy attack? Most fighters of World War II were fully expected to take-off from grass. Only later were makeshift runways required for some heavily laden fighter-bombers battling for the return of occupied land. Although many jets were, and are, capable of take-off from grass, to get away from a reliance on runways was considered high priority by some nations. Also, using other methods of take-off would naturally extend an air force's operational capability. The goal of being able to hide a fighter in woodland, advance with front line forces despite the state of the ground, or fly a jet fighter from water or from a naval vessel not equipped with a long deck appeared worth the expense of development.

Experimentation in the latter 1940s and early 1950s to these ends covered principally three forms. *The first*, and a concept of fighting that had originated during World War I, was the development of a flying-boat fighter, only this time to be jet powered. Several countries were attracted to this, the chief exponents being Britain and the USA.

The British aircraft was the Saunders-Roe SR.A/1, which had been designed to specification E.6/44 and first flew on 16 July 1947. A wonderful feat of engineering, it was the world's first turbojet-powered flying-boat and the first flying-boat to exceed 805 km/h (500 mph) in level flight. The first of three prototypes was powered by two Metropolitan-Vickers Beryl M.V.B.I. engines, each rated at 1,474 kg (3,250 lb) thrust. The wings were straight but employed a high-speed aerofoil section, and housed semi-retractable stabilising floats. Armament comprised four 20 mm cannon in the nose. After extensive testing, it was decided reluctantly that the bulky hull diminished both manoeuvrability and speed and the project was abandoned. But to spectators at a Farnborough air show, the sight of an SR.A/1 flying low and fast upside-down over the airstrip gave little indication of this.

To solve the same problem of a water-based jet fighter, Convair in the USA adopted a completely different approach. First flying on 9 April 1953, its Sea Dart was a delta-winged aircraft, evolved to float in the water prior to and during the initial phase of take-off. A retractable hydroski was then lowered which, at a particular speed, gave sufficient hydrodynamic lift to raise the aircraft above the water, where it aquaplaned until take-off. By retracting the hydroski after take-off, the clean aerodynamic lines were retained. The problem of a flying-boat's bulky hull had been solved.

The first Sea Dart was eventually followed by three others, only one of which was flown. In August 1954 the second became the first sea-going aircraft to exceed the speed of sound (in a shallow dive), but was destroyed in an accident three months later. More powerful than the first, this aircraft used two Westinghouse J46 turbojets, each rated at 2,720 kg (6,000 lb) thrust. Despite promising results, this programme was also cancelled, with the result that no jet-powered flying-boat or seaplane fighter has ever become operational.

*The second* concept was, at this time, dominated by America. The search for a realistic vertical take-off fighter, using the engine technology available, proved immensely difficult. Only in hindsight do we know that it took Hawker Siddeley of Britain and its Kestrel/Harrier to meet the demands of a successful VTOL warplane. As chapter four covers VTOL aeroplanes of all types, it is sufficient in this chapter to say that these two countries first settled on tail-sitting and ramp-launched designs respectively. If it points upwards, it must go up!

In 1950 the US Navy held a design competition for an aircraft which could be used as an escort fighter, able to take-off, fight and land without the need for a long aircraft carrier deck. Eventually Convair and Lockheed constructed prototypes for testing, the XFY-1 Pogo and the XFV-1 Vertical Riser respectively. Using specially developed handling equipment to raise them to vertical position, the prototypes first flew in 1954, the XFY-1 on 2 August and the XFV-1 on 16 June. Both types rested upright on castor wheels and were each powered by a 5,850 ehp Allison YT40-A turbo-prop engine in the nose driving two 4.88 m (16 ft) diameter Curtiss-Wright turbo-electric co-axial contra-rotating propellers. The pilot of each aircraft sat on a gimballed seat, which enabled him to tilt at 45° when the aircraft was in vertical position.

Trials with the XFV-1 were performed in horizontal flight, but this aircraft was never flown vertically. Eventually the Navy cancelled further development. It was put on display at the Los Alamitos Naval Air Station, where it remained for many years. Recently, Lockheed repainted and refurbished the XFV-1 and it now has a place of honour at the San Diego Aerospace Museum.

The more successful XFY-1 made some 280 tethered 'flights', using a special test rig constructed in a 59.4 m (195 ft) high airship hangar, before making a free vertical take-off and landing in August. Seventy more free 'up and down' verti-

**SNECMA C.450 Coléoptère**

cal flights culminated, on 2 November 1954, with a transition from vertical to horizontal and vice versa. Sadly, this aircraft was later also abandoned by the Navy.

Interestingly, in France a similar VTOL concept was tested using the SNECMA C.450 Coléoptère, not in itself built as a prototype operational aircraft but instead to research the technology for a possible follow-up design. Its special features included an annular wing of light alloy construction, made up of two skins and internal structure. Retractable foreplanes were mounted in the nose and cruciform swivelling fins provided directional control in all axes for normal horizontal flight. Like the American aircraft, the Coléoptère rested on castor wheels but was powered by a rear-mounted SNECMA Atar 101E.V turbojet engine rated at 3,700 kg (8,157 lb) thrust.

**Lockheed XFV-1 Vertical Riser**    (*Lockheed*)

**McDonnell XF-85 Goblin**    (*McDonnell Douglas*)

**Upper-rear view of the XF-85 Goblin**    (*McDonnell Douglas*)

**Sud-Est S.E. 5000 Baroudeur on its
rocket-powered trolley**

Earlier tests with pilotless and piloted 'Atar Volant' vehicles had proved the basic Coléoptère concept of vertical flight, with directional control at take-off and landing by means of pneumatic deflection of the main jet efflux. The Coléoptère made its first free flight at Melun-Villaroche on 6 May 1959, but on 25 July the aircraft went out of control and crashed from 75 m (250 ft) during a transition from vertical to horizontal flight. Luckily, the pilot's tilting seat could be ejected and he survived the accident which destroyed the Coléoptère. Despite the crash the experiments were considered a success, although testing of all tail-sitters ended.

*The third* concept adopted a rocket-powered trolley or retractable skids for take-off, relying on the skids for landing. One exponent was the French-built Sud-Est S.E.5000 Baroudeur tactical support fighter, first flown on 1 August 1953. Powered by a SNECMA Atar 101C turbojet, it demonstrated its ability to take-off from snow-covered, frozen and muddy ground, fields and beaches, and more-powerful pre-production examples were actually built for service trials. Maximum speed achieved was 1,195 km/h (742 mph). Of course the independent rocket-powered trolley method was not new, a similar approach having been tested by Arado during

World War II for its Ar 234 Blitz jet recon-naissance-bomber.

On a completely different tack, McDonnell produced the XF-85 Goblin parasite fighter, the smallest jet-propelled fighter ever built. Designed as part of the defence system of the Consolidated-Vultee (Convair) B-36 strategic bomber, itself a unique aircraft with six pusher-mounted engines in the trailing-edges of the huge 70 m (230 ft) span wings, it had folding wings spanning just 6.47 m (21 ft 2¾ in) and a length of 4.53 m (14 ft 10½ in) to enable it to fit into the forward bomb-bay of the B-36. Six tail surfaces were spaced round the rear fuselage. Power was provided by a Westinghouse 24C (J34-WE-22) turbojet engine rated at 1,361 kg (3,000 lb) thrust. As it was intended to be launched and retrieved in the air by the B-36 using a hook-on 'trapeze' technique, no under-carriage was fitted as standard, although for flight testing emergency skids were provided. In the event it was just as well. Having been taken aloft previously (but not released) for captive tests, the XF-85 made its first free flight on 23 August 1948. The carrier aircraft or 'motherplane' for the tests was a specially converted Boeing B-29. However, when the time came for the fighter to hook back onto the B-29's lowered trap-eze at an altitude of 7,620 m (25,000 ft), rough air caused all sorts of problems. Suddenly the trap-eze struck the Plexiglas canopy of the XF-85, smashing it and knocking the helmet and oxygen mask off the pilot. With tremendous presence of mind the pilot put what remained of the oxygen hose in his mouth and made a successful emergency landing on the skids at nearly 275 km/h (170 mph). Because the fighter proved unstable in flight, wing-mounted fins were

**Sud-Est S.E. 5000 Baroudeur using parachute-brake during landing**

**Convair B-36** *(General Dynamics)*
**Rockwell International XFV-12A**

**Saunders-Roe S-R.53**

added. Three 'hook-ons' were subsequently achieved, the first on 14 October 1948. All was looking good for the fighter, its speed of 837 km/h (520 mph) considered slightly low but adequate to ward off potential enemy fighters from a B-36 performing a long-range mission, but unfortunately the use of a parasite fighter in the production B-36 was later rejected.

Another revolutionary warplane that nearly achieved production was the British Saunders-Roe S-R.53 interceptor. Given that its first flight date was 16 May 1957, it had an incredible estimated maximum speed of more than Mach 2.4 in developed form. Its secret lay in the power plant, a mixed unit combining a 3,630 kg (8,000 lb) thrust de Havilland Spectre variable-thrust long-life rocket motor and a 795 kg (1,750 lb) thrust Armstrong Siddeley Viper turbojet. A higher-powered version for naval use was being constructed as the S-R.177 when, in December 1957, the contract was cancelled in favour of the possible future deployment of surface-to-air missiles.

As a conclusion to this chapter it is possible to come right up to date and include a fantastic flying machine of the '80s. The Rockwell International XFV-12A single-seater was designed for the US Navy's V/STOL Fighter/Attack Technology

Prototype programme, which calls for a V/STOL aircraft capable of operation from comparatively small carrier decks that would have neither catapult nor arrester gear. This aircraft employs the augmentor-wing concept with forward canard and aft semi-delta wings, and is powered by a special version of the Pratt & Whitney F401-PW-400 advanced technology turbofan engine. Estimated maximum speed exceeds Mach 2.

Tethered testing of the XFV-12A in the hover mode, using a NASA gantry, began in 1978, but more recently the development programme has been constrained by funding limitations. Interestingly, this aircraft uses a method of propulsion for vertical flying very similar in concept to that of the Lockheed Hummingbird research aircraft. For vertical take-off, a special electro-hydraulically actuated diverter valve installed in the tailpipe of the engine (which remains open for normal horizontal flight) closes, causing the exhaust gases from the engine to be diverted through ducts to nozzles in the wings and canards. A full-span ejector-flap system on each wing and canard allows free air to be drawn over the flaps and ejected downward, the ambient air and exhaust together giving the required jet-lift.

# 3. The Flying Wings

Incredible as it may seem, flying wing aircraft nearly became operational with the Luftwaffe in 1945 as Gotha Go 229s and again with the USAF in the late 1940s as Northrop B-49s.

The first chapter includes reference to tailless aircraft, but the term flying wing is generally accepted to mean aircraft with no tail surfaces or fuselage and with the power plant (if fitted) and crew accommodated within the contours of the aerofoil so that there are no portions of the aircraft which do not contribute directly to lift, with the exception of the propeller shaft housings. Within these bounds the Dunne biplanes of the 'stick and string' era or any similar aircraft cannot be said to have originated the concept, while the French Fauvel A.V.2 of 1933 met all the criteria for

a powered flying wing except for its 40 hp ABC Scorpion engine which was mounted on struts above the wing. So where are the beginnings?

The American Northrop company certainly claims to have developed the world's first successful flying wing aircraft in its N-1M, which first flew in the summer of 1940. Built as an 11.59 m (38 ft) span experimental model for a much larger twin-engined transport, it made more than 200 successful flights and was the forerunner of the later Flying Wing bombers. It was fitted first with down-turned wingtips, which took the place of conventional vertical control surfaces, but was found to be too stable in flight and was therefore modified. Without doubt the N-1M was the first fully successful piloted and powered flying wing,

**Northrop N-1M**

but some doubt must be expressed as to it being the first successful flying wing of any type, bearing in mind the experiments of Reimar and Walter Horten in Germany during the 1930s.

Having test flown models, the Horten brothers began work on their first full-size flying wing glider in 1931, the pilot adopting a prone position in keeping with the thickness of the wing. Although the Ho 1 flew several times, it was not a success and was discarded. Four Ho II gliders followed, one of which was later fitted with an 80 hp Hirth engine and pusher propeller in 1935. Among those who officially tested the powered aircraft was the famed woman pilot Hanna Reitsch. Ho IIIs, Ho IV and Ho VI were all built as gliders, while the first and important Ho V was completed in 1938 as a powered two-seater with two Hirth engines.

Powered by two 240 hp Argus As 10 engines, the Ho VII was originally considered suitable for pilot training duties, but in the event remained a prototype. Therefore, there is little doubt that the most successful Horten flying wing was the Ho IX. Envisaged as a single-seat day fighter, two-seat night fighter and subsequently a fighter-bomber, the first prototype of the Ho IX was completed as a glider, the second and third as powered single-seaters, while a fourth was under construction as a two-seater when the Gotha works (Gotha having taken over the aircraft for production purposes as the Go 229) was overrun by the Allies. According to the 1945–46 *Jane's*, the Ho IX had a welded steel tube centre-section, wood outer sections and metal tips. All control surfaces were on the outer wings. Divided hinged surfaces were responsible for

**Horten Ho IX V3**   *(Harold G. Martin)*

**I.A.38**

longitudinal and lateral control and spoilers for directional control. The proposed armament was four 30 mm MK 108 cannon for the day fighter, with provision for 1,000 kg (2,200 lb) of bombs when used as a fighter-bomber. The night fighter would have had heavy calibre guns and rockets.

A seemingly unrelated aircraft, first flown on 9 December 1960, was the Argentinian I.A.38 experimental tailless cargo aircraft, capable of accommodating 6 tons of cargo within the 32 m (105 ft) wing and below. Fins and balanced rudders were fitted near the wingtips, while the fuselage was incorporated in and below the wing. Power was provided by four I.A.16EI Gaucho radial engines, rated at 450 hp each, driving pusher propellers. Maximum speed was estimated at 252 km/h (156 mph). Designed by Dr Reimar Horten, it had been based on his wartime Ho VIII, a projected 60-passenger flying wing aircraft to be powered by six 600 hp BMW engines with pusher propellers. The prototype I.A.38 was completed in 1959 but flight trials were delayed because of cooling problems with the engines. Once flying had begun it quickly

became obvious that the aircraft was unsuitable for its designed task and was abandoned.

Britain too became interested in the concept of a six-jet tailless transport aircraft, and it was to obtain the data necessary to determine the final configuration of such an aircraft that Armstrong Whitworth produced the A.W.52 to Specification E.9/44, having previously flown the A.W.52G glider. With a wing similar in plan to the Horten Ho V, the A.W.52 had a centre section with sweptback leading-edge and two tapered and sweptback outer sections. Longitudinal and lateral control was by 'controllers' (elevons), hinged on each outer wing to serve as both elevators and ailerons. Controllers were hinged to movable surfaces known as 'correctors', which provided fore-and-aft trim and were used to counteract pitching caused by the lowering and raising of the flaps. Twin elliptical fins and rudders for directional control were mounted on the wingtips, while anti-spin chutes were carried in wingtip containers. Two A.W.52s were built, the first with two Rolls-Royce Nene turbojets and the second with two Rolls-Royce Derwent 5 turbojets,

**Armstrong Whitworth A.W. 52**

each engine rated at 2,270 kg (5,000 lb) thrust and 1,588 kg (3,500 lb) thrust respectively. The first flew initially on 13 November 1947 and was subsequently abandoned after an accident on 30 May 1949. The second aircraft completed its research programme, but the full-size transport did not follow.

For the most important flying wing aircraft, however, we have to return to the USA and John K. Northrop. Prior to the forming of Northrop Aircraft Inc in 1939, J.K. Northrop and W.K. Kay had formed (in 1928) the Avion Corporation of Burbank, California. This concern produced a powered aircraft which incorporated flying wing features, although it had a conventional tail unit supported by twin booms. Interestingly, the pilot was accommodated in a cockpit in the wing. Commercial difficulties restricted development of this aircraft, but with the founding of Northrop Aircraft the concept received a 'shot in the arm'.

Northrop's first purely all-wing aircraft was the N-1M, originally powered by two 65 hp Lycoming engines and later by two 120 hp Franklins. Such was its success that preliminary layout of a long-range flying wing bomber was submitted to the USAAF as early as September 1941. With the assistance and co-operation of the Wright Field Engineering Division, actual work on the projected bomber began in 1942. Design of the full-size mock-up was approved in July of the following year.

Four twin-engined flying scale models of the projected XB-35 bomber, of about one-third size, were built to obtain data useful for the detailed design of the bomber and to familiarise pilots with this new type of aircraft. These aircraft, designated N-9M, had a span of 18.29 m (60 ft). The first two were powered by 275 hp Menasco engines with pusher propellers, as was the third aircraft designated N-9M-A, but the fourth, the N-9M-B, had two 300 hp Franklins. Each N-9M had an all-up weight of about 3,221 kg (7,100 lb). The N-9Ms flew for several hundred hours.

Work on the XB-35 prototype was started in early 1943 at Northrop's Hawthorne plant and was completed in 1946. The 52.43 m (172 ft) straight-tapered and sweptback aluminium alloy wing was constructed in one piece. Drag-

**Above:** Northrop N-9M   (*Northrop*)

**Below:** Northrop YB-35   (*US Air Force*)

**Northrop YB-35** (*Northrop*)

**Layout of the Northrop B-35** (*Northrop*)

**Northrop YB-49**    *(Northrop)*

inducing double-split flaps were fitted at the wingtips for directional control, with elevons between these and the outer engines. Fixed wingtip slots in the leading-edge opened only at speeds approaching the stall. The crew of seven was accommodated in a fuselage nacelle constructed around the centreline of the wing. The pilot was situated in the forward cockpit offset to port with a bubble canopy, the bombardier to starboard with bombing windows in the leading edge. Bunks were provided for six reserve crew members. Two Pratt & Whitney R-4360-17 and two R-4360-21 Wasp Major radial piston engines, rated at 3,000 hp each, were fitted in the trailing-edge, driving Hamilton Standard four-blade reversible-pitch pusher propellers. Defensive armament comprised two electrically-operated four-gun turrets, one above and one below the wing, and four electrically-operated remotely-controlled two-gun turrets, one above and one below each outer wing section, with a

fire control blister positioned towards the end of the central nacelle. Maximum take-off weight was up to 94,800 kg (209,000 lb).

First flying on 25 June 1946 (actually its delivery flight from Hawthorne to Muroc – now Edwards Air Force Base), it was put through extensive trials before fourteen development aircraft were ordered as YB-35s. Two of the YB-35s were subsequently earmarked for conversion to YB-49 standard, the first YB-49 flying on 21 October 1947. Basically similar to the YB-35s, each YB-49 was powered by eight 1,814 kg (4,000 lb) thrust Allison J-35 turbojet engines, mounted in two groups of four each side of the central nacelle and exhausting at the trailing-edge. Air intakes were positioned in the leading-edge.

In 1948 thirty production B-49s were ordered for the Air Force, but these were cancelled in January of the following year. In February 1949 a YB-49 flew from Muroc AFB to Washington DC, a

**Northrop YB-49**    *(US Air Force)*

THE NORTHROP
*Flying Wing Jet Bomber*
YB·49

**Layout of the Northrop YB-49** *(Northrop)*
**The projected Flying Wing airliner, based on the B-49** *(Northrop)*

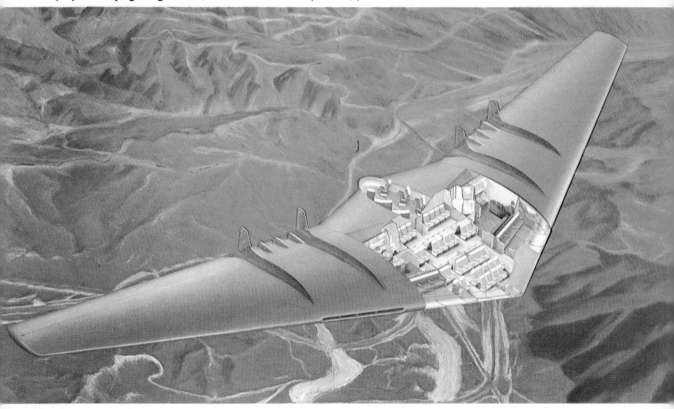

*Left:* **Northrop YB-49** *(Northrop)*

**Northrop XRB-49A**

**Northrop MX-324 with rocket motor**

**Northrop XP-79 Flying Ram**

distance of 3,633 km (2,258 miles), at an average speed of 822 km/h (511 mph). On another occasion a YB-49 remained airborne for 9 hours 30 minutes at altitudes ranging from 10,670 m to 12,200 m (35,000 ft to 40,000 ft), during which it covered a distance of 5,565 km (3,458 miles) at an average cruising speed of 615 km/h (382 mph).

After the B-49s had been cancelled, Northrop was asked to convert a third YB-35 to jet standard, but this time as the six-jet YRB-49A reconnaissance-bomber. First flown on 4 May 1950, it had four engines in the trailing-edge and two in external pods below and forward of the wing. This became the sole survivor of the flying wing series. A commercial airliner version of the B-49 was also planned, accommodating about 48 passengers and with a rest lounge and galley.

Interestingly, the story of Northrop's involvement with flying wings has not as yet been fully related, and for two more important aircraft the clock has to be turned back to 1944. In that year Northrop completed in strict secrecy the conversion of its MX-324 glider to carry an Aerojet XCAL-200 rocket motor which used as fuel monoethylaniline oxidised with red fuming nitric acid. The first powered flight was made on 5 July,

and as such this aircraft became America's first military rocket plane to fly. News of these experiments was not released until 1947. From the MX-324 was developed the incredible XP-79 Flying Ram, which made its one and only flight on 12 September 1945. Undoubtedly one of the shortest-lived aircraft, it was built as an experimental flying wing fighter, intended primarily for slicing off the tail units of enemy bombers, although four 0.50 in machine-guns were fitted. The wing was constructed of welded heavy magnesium plate to withstand the impact. Power was provided by two 522 kg (1,150 lb) thrust Westinghouse turbojet engines, which allowed a maximum speed of about 821 km/h (510 mph). As with the MX-324, the pilot lay in a prone position in the centreline cockpit. Bellows-operated split horizontal control surfaces were located in the outer wings, air for their actuation being diverted by control valves in the oval tunnel ducts which formed the wingtips. Unfortunately, after flying for about fifteen minutes the aircraft went out of control and was destroyed.

Today, only a handful of gliders and ultralights keep alive any measure of the flying wing concept.

# 4. Up and Away

It is probably true to say that more money and effort have gone into the quest for successful vertical take-off and landing (VTOL) aeroplanes since the war, to less effect, than almost any other branch of aviation research. Arguably, the main reason for failure has all too often been the designers' predilection for making the aircraft, or the method by which VTOL is achieved, too complicated. In the world today there are only two operational VTOL aeroplanes (also capable of short take-off and landing – STOL), the British Harrier and the Soviet . Yak-36. The Harrier entered service first and uses the thrust from its single Rolls-Royce turbofan engine to achieve vertical and horizontal flight by pointing rotatable exhaust nozzles either downward or aft. An over simplification, perhaps, but it proves the point.

As this chapter is not so concerned with the history of VTOL as with some of the more unusual aircraft that have been built and flown, the

**Hawker Siddeley P.1127 Kestrel, prototype of the Harrier**   (*British Aerospace*)

**Bell XV-15**

selected types are not necessarily in chronological order, particularly where several products of a single manufacturer can be grouped easily. Reference should be made also to the Bachem Ba 349 Natter in the first chapter and Convair, Lockheed, Rockwell International and SNECMA types in chapter two.

In 1935 the Bell Aircraft Corporation was founded and in 1937 produced its first original design, a long-range escort monoplane with two engines driving pusher propellers and designated the XFM-1 Airacuda. In October 1942 this young company test flew its XP-59A Airacomet at a secret base at Muroc to record the first flight of an American jet fighter, and on 14 October 1947

its rocket-powered X-1 research aircraft became the first aeroplane to fly faster than the speed of sound. Although the X-1 was undoubtedly the most important research aircraft ever produced by Bell, many later types continued the pioneering tradition.

In the context of VTOL, Bell has investigated several methods of vertical flight; jet deflection, tilting duct, tilting rotor, flying belt and rocket platform are included here, helicopters forming the next chapter. The first of these was the XV-3, a tilting-rotor convertiplane. Becoming the world's first tilting-rotor, fixed-wing aircraft to achieve 100% tilting of its rotors, it proved the design practicable. Built under a US Army-USAF con-

**Bell XV-3**

tract, it had two combination rotor/propellers mounted near the tips of the fixed wings. These operated as rotors during take-off, landing and low-speed flight, tilting to a forward-facing position for horizontal cruise and high-speed flight once lift had been transferred to the wings. Power for the rotors was provided by a single 450 hp Pratt & Whitney R-985 piston engine located behind the cabin, electric motors being used to tilt the rotors/propellers. The cabin itself accommodated four persons.

The first XV-3 made its first vertical flight on 23 August 1955, and had successfully performed 15° conversions in flight before it crash landed on 25 October 1956. Full-scale wind tunnel tests preceded the resumption of flying with the second XV-3. The first full conversion from vertical to horizontal flight, and vice versa, was therefore not carried out until 18 December 1958. By 1961 a great many operating hours had been logged at speeds ranging from 24 km/h (15 mph) rearward to 291 km/h (181 mph) in forward flight and at altitudes from sea level to 3,660 m (12,000 ft).

More than 110 full conversions were performed and the aircraft was evaluated by NASA. The results obtained encouraged NASA to award Bell a modification contract in February 1962, covering design, development and evaluation of engineering changes to the rotor system to improve high-speed stability and control of the convertiplane. However, the XV-3 remained in a hangar for about three years while engineers worked on a solution. During May 1966 twenty-five test runs were conducted successfully, but the aircraft was subsequently damaged when a pylon mounting failed. Over the span of its career the XV-3 type achieved more than 250 flights.

A direct result of the XV-3 programme is the XV-15, two examples of which are currently flying in a research programme to explore the limits of the operational flight envelope and assess the aircraft's application to military and civil transport needs.

The XV-15s airframe structure is basically that of a conventional aeroplane. However, wingtip-mounted 1,550 shp Avco Lycoming LTC1K-4K turboshaft engines actually rotate with the rotors/propellers from vertical to horizontal position and vice versa. For hover flight the wing trailing-edge flaps and flap/ailerons (flaperons) are deflected downward to reduce the wing download, thereby increasing hovering efficiency. Hover roll control is provided by differential rotor collective pitch, pitch control by cyclic pitch, and yaw control by differential cyclic pitch. Dual controls for use in the helicopter mode are similar to those of a conventional rotating-wing aircraft. Therefore, dual collective control sticks provide power and collective pitch for altitude control, and dual control columns provide longitudinal and lateral control: dual rudder pedals provide directional control. In the aeroplane flight mode, the control columns and rudder pedals are employed conventionally, while the collective stick/power lever continues in use for power management.

The first XV-15 made its initial free hovering flight on 3 May 1977, and in June the following year began wind tunnel tests at NASA's Ames Research Center. In April 1979 the second aircraft began flight tests in helicopter mode, and just over three months later, on 24 July, it performed the first full in-flight conversion to aeroplane mode. Subsequent tests included flights at 1,525 m (5,000 ft) with in-flight conversions at speeds up to 384 km/h (238 mph). Following inspection the second aircraft has continued test flying, on 17 June 1980 demonstrating high-speed cruise flight at 557 km/h (346 mph).

In July 1979 Bell Helicopter announced the receipt of a contract from NASA covering preliminary design study of an advanced rotor blade for use on the XV-15. The goal is to produce eventually a composite rotor blade that will offer improved performance and extended life. Future military and commercial aircraft which might be derived from the XV-15 would have a wing span of about 10.67 m (35 ft) and fuselage length of 12.50 m (41 ft), enabling accommodation of 15 troops or 12 passengers. Maximum level speed of the XV-15 is estimated to be 615 km/h (382 mph), and a range of 824 km (512 miles) is being quoted.

Changing from convertiplane (with the XV-3) to more conventional aeroplane configuration, Bell produced the X-14 under a USAF contract. Of simple design with an open cockpit, straight wings and two Bristol Siddeley Viper turbojet

**Bell X-14**

**Bell Rocket Belt**

engines mounted side-by-side in the fuselage nose, the X-14 used jet deflection to achieve VTOL, thrust diverters mounted behind the engines deflecting the jet efflux towards the ground during take-off and landing, or rearward for forward thrust. Compressed air nozzles at the wingtips and tail provided directional and stability control for low-speed flying or hovering.

The X-14 made its first hovering flight on 19 February 1957 and first transition from hovering to forward flight on 24 May 1958. Flying in original form continued until mid-1960, when the Viper engines were replaced by General Electric J85s under NASA direction to evaluate the J85 for VTOL applications. Accommodating a pilot only, the X-14 had a maximum speed of about 257 km/h (160 mph).

Seemingly inspired by tales of fantasy, many pilots have longed to leave the confines of the cockpit and experience the unencumbered flight of the bird. Ultralights or minimum aircraft (as found in the seventh chapter) have fulfilled this role for many, but for a few experimentation has brought the dream much closer.

For serious applications Bell developed the SRLD (Small Rocket Lift Device), better remembered as the Rocket Belt. Conceived by Bell Aerosystems' engineer Wendell F. Moore in 1953, it is said that his first drawings were sketched out in the Californian desert sands near Edwards Air Force Base. His idea was to strap a rocket motor directly onto the back of a man to produce an integrated flying system.

Prior to the construction of a Rocket Belt, Bell

built a test rig simulator to investigate stability and other problems. The main element consisted of a simple harness for the 'pilot' with two downward-facing exhaust nozzles, linked by tubing to a nitrogen gas supply. By increasing the gas supply flowing through the nozzles, the ground engineer was able to lift the 'pilot'. Testing began in 1958. One outcome was to move the nozzles further from the 'pilot's' body, the jacket sleeves of one operator having been destroyed by the downward blast.

By this time the US Army had become interested in the project, and a design study contract was awarded to Aerojet-General for a suitable engine to power the Rocket Belt proper. The Army saw the device as useful for several military applications, including flying over barbed wire, rivers and mine fields, reconnaissance, counter-guerrilla warfare, assault, perimeter guard and amphibious landings. Bell also envisaged its civil potential, perhaps for powerline and pipeline patrols, rescue operations and surveillance. A contract to construct the SRLD was awarded to Bell in August 1960 by the US Army Transportation, Research and Engineering Command.

Using the 127 kg (280 lb) thrust rocket motor developed by Aerojet-General, Bell constructed an SRLD. The pilot varied the thrust by means of a squeeze throttle on the right-hand arm rest. Yaw control was achieved by 'jetavator' gas deflectors, operated by levers located on the left arm rest. The test programme began with the unmanned SRLD strapped to a tethering rig, in order to fire the engine and work the controls from a remote position. Finally it was decided that Moore could attempt a tethered 'flight' wearing protective clothing. In the course of later tethered 'flights', perhaps reaching an altitude of 3.2 m (10 ft), Moore occasionally cut his motor in order to regain stability after testing the jetavators, allowing the tethering line attached to the top of the SRLD to lower him to the ground. Unknown to anyone this line was shearing with use. On one 'flight', when Moore switched off the motor, the line was not able to carry the weight and broke. It was a cruel turn of fate for Moore, who was now out of action for the first free flight test.

Another pilot was found and underwent a series of 56 tethered flights to become familiar with the SRLD and eliminate the final minor prob-

**Bell Jet Belt**  (*Bell Helicopter Textron*)

**Williams Wasp**

lems. All was now set for the 'big one'. In the cold morning air of 20 April 1961 Harold Graham, the new pilot, donned the SRLD and gave the motor a short, sharp test blast to ensure all was working. Then, squeezing the throttle control, he lifted 0.45 m (1 ft 6 in) off the ground in free flight, gradually moving forward at a speed of a few mph. This flight lasted no more than 13 seconds, but had proved correct Moore's belief in the concept.

Subsequent flights by several pilots demonstrated the SRLD's ability to make controlled flights of 262 m (860 ft) distance, achieving speeds of nearly 97 km/h (60 mph) and altitudes of 18.5 m (60 ft). In October 1961 a special Rocket Belt flight was performed for President John F. Kennedy, the pilot launching himself from an amphibious craft and flying across water to land precisely in front of the President. Altogether hundreds of demonstration flights were made, a special Rocket Belt demonstration team visiting fairs and other meetings throughout the USA and in Canada, Mexico and France. It was the highlight of the US National Exhibition in Mexico City, where more than 620,000 people saw the Rocket Belt during 28 flights in seven days.

But this is only half the story. As a follow-up to its SRLD or Rocket Belt, Bell Aerosystems developed and flight tested one-man and two-man flying platforms for possible use on the earth and the moon. Known as Pogos, each machine consisted of a simple open platform structure, mounted on four castoring wheels and carrying Rocket Belt propulsion systems. The two-man Pogo had an endurance of 21 seconds. The pilot stood on the vehicle's rear platform and flew the machine by controlling the rocket nozzles with hand, arm and shoulder movements. By mid-June 1967 the two-man Pogo had made 27 flights, carrying passengers weighing from 52 to 86 kg (115 to 190 lb). Eventually, Bell's kinesthetic control system had virtually eliminated all manual control, the pilot being required only to vary thrust and lean in the direction he wished to travel.

One of the major problems with rocket-powered machines was their extremely short endurance. If a Pogo was to find its way to the moon one day, an advanced version with refuelling capability would need to be developed. However, for travel on the earth it was decided

**Bell X-22A**  (*Bell Helicopter Textron*)

that the Pogo would be better suited to small turbojet engines of the kind under development at that time for the Jet Belt.

As mentioned above, the Rocket Belt worked well but had a limited endurance by virtue of its rocket propulsion system. Therefore, Bell developed for the US Army, under contract of the DOD's Advanced Research Projects Agency, a similar back-pack using a single Williams Research Corporation WR-19 high-bypass turbojet engine as the Jet Belt. An interesting design feature was that the pilot had a helmet vibrator which warned him when fuel contents had reached reserve level. The first flight was achieved on 7 April 1969. It was hoped event-

ually to realise an endurance of up to 26 minutes with the Jet Belt. Unfortunately it never achieved operational status with the US Army.

On 26 January 1970, the Bell Aerospace Company Division of Textron Inc announced that it had granted to Williams Research Corporation a licence to manufacture, use and sell certain small lift device systems in the US and Canada. These included the Jet Belt. However, Williams Research appear to have concentrated more on the Pogo system, for on 14 February 1974 it announced that it had tested successfully an advanced two-man flying platform known as the Wasp, powered by one 317 kg (700 lb) thrust Williams WR-19-9 miniature turbofan engine.

**McDonnell XV-1**

Essentially a platform with the engine mounted vertically, it had a maximum speed potential of 97 km/h (60 mph). The flight tests were conducted on a tethered line, under a US Navy contract to demonstrate its suitability to meet a US Marine Corps STAMP (Small Tactical Aerial Mobility Platform) requirement. In the event this vehicle too was not adopted for service.

The largest of Bell's V/STOL aeroplanes was the Model D2127, better known under its US Navy designation X-22A. Designed as a tilting-duct research aircraft, it was powered by four 1,250 shp General Electric YT58-GE-8D turbo-shaft engines mounted in pairs at the root of each wing. The wings themselves were at the rear of the fuselage, each with a tilting duct built into the leading-edge and with an elevon control surface in the slipstream from the duct. A large fixed vertical fin was fitted at the tail. Foreplanes at the front of the square-section fuselage carried two forward ducts, with elevons as on the wings. Cross-shafting of the engines ensured that all ducted propellers continued to be powered in the event of an engine failing. Control of the X-22A was achieved at the ducts through thrust modulation, by changing the propeller pitch, and by the elevons. By increasing or decreasing the power output of the engines, altitude control was achieved.

Two X-22As were built to US Navy contract for tri-service research, the first making its maiden flight on 17 March 1966. Before a heavy landing on 8 August caused this aircraft to be abandoned, it had performed four vertical flights to a height of 7.6 m (25 ft), turned through 180°, performed STOL take-offs and flown at 161 km/h (100 mph) in forward flight. Its maximum level speed, however, was estimated to be 510 km/h (316 mph).

**Ryan X-13 Vertijet**   (*Teledyne Ryan Aeronautical*)

The second X-22A first flew on 26 January the following year. By May 1969 this had accumulated the impressive totals of 386 vertical and 216 short take-offs, resulting in 405 vertical and 197 short landings. Further, no fewer than 185 transitions from vertical to horizontal flight and vice versa had been made. Such was its success that in 1968 it was fitted with a variable stability system designed and built by the Cornell Aeronautical Laboratory. With this installed the X-22A could change its flight characteristics automatically while airborne. Tests continued for several more years, finally under the direction of the Cornell Aeronautical Laboratory.

Bell was certainly not alone in the experimental convertiplane field during the 1950s, McDonnell for one flying its own XV-1 before the Bell XV-3 had left the ground. The two convertiplanes were also very different. Whereas Bell had chosen tilting rotors, McDonnell fitted a 550 hp Continental R-975-19

piston engine in the rear fuselage to drive two compressors to supply air to the rotor-tip pressure-jets during vertical flight and to turn the rear-mounted propeller during forward flight. Fuel was fed to the rotor-tip burners through a rotary fuel governor driven from the rotor hub accessory drive. There were also two small anti-torque tail rotors. In operation the jet-driven rotor lifted the aircraft in vertical flight, the wings and the rear-mounted propeller taking over for forward cruise flight during which the rotor autorotated at its lowest drag configuration.

A joint development of McDonnell Aircraft Corporation, the Wright Air Development Center, USAF, and the Transportation Corps of the US Army, the XV-1 was first flown on 11 February 1954. A second XV-1 flew on 14 July but was damaged during power-off autorotation landing trials on 10 December. However, the first aircraft achieved a full conversion from vertical to horizontal flight on 29 April 1955. Before development of the XV-1 ended in 1957, one of the aircraft had flown at 322 km/h (200 mph).

Rivalled only by Bell in the extent of its VTOL research during the 1940s, 1950s and 1960s, Ryan produced three very different aircraft in its Verti series – Vertijet, Vertiplane and Vertifan. The first of these to fly, but as a conventional aeroplane with a fixed tricycle landing gear, was the X-13 Vertijet, on 10 December 1955. Powered by a 4,535 kg (10,000 lb) thrust Rolls-Royce Avon turbojet engine, it had high-set delta wings with small fins at the tips and a large vertical fin and rudder. Although for the first flight the initial X-13 built was given a fixed undercarriage, no undercarriage was to be standard, the aircraft taking off instead from a mobile ground servicing support trailer, the bed of which was raised hydraulically to a vertical position so that the aircraft was suspended in a nose-up attitude by a hook under the forward fuselage. As with the Convair and Lockheed tail-sitting fighters (see the second chapter), the pilot was provided with a pivoted seat.

The X-13 was the culmination of work begun in 1947. Then Ryan had mounted an Allison J-33 engine on a horizontal test stand to research methods of varying the jet thrust for directional control. For the next stage in development the engine was mounted on a vertical test rig, finally being fitted with a cockpit, controls and delta wings for manned trials. Such was the success of these experiments that the USAF awarded Ryan a contract in 1953 to construct the X-13.

Following initial trials the first X-13 had the fixed landing gear removed and another temporary structure fitted, this time a tubular unit to allow the aircraft to be tested in a tail-sitting attitude. In this form the X-13 flew on 28 May 1956. Hook-on trials, using a nylon rope stretched between two steel towers, followed. Meanwhile the second X-13 had been completed and this aircraft first flew on 28 November 1956, performing a transition from horizontal flight to hovering flight. On 11 April 1957 the second X-13 completed the first sequence of vertical take-off, transition to horizontal cruising flight and return for a vertical landing, and both aircraft finished their test programmes successfully. Today, the X-13s are displayed in US museums.

In its fully developed form, the X-13 could be hovered and manoeuvred near the ground,

controlled by deflection of its exhaust and thrust variations. Conventional control surfaces were provided for horizontal flight. The single seat X-13 had a wing span of 6.40 m (21 ft) and a length of 7.32 m (24 ft). Maximum T-O weight was about 3,401 kg (7,500 lb).

Three years after the first flight of the Vertijet Ryan flew the VZ-3RY Vertiplane, built for the US Army under the technical direction of the Office of Naval Research. It was a simply constructed V/STOL research monoplane of fairly conventional high-wing configuration, but with very extensive double retractable wing flaps which extended far below and to the rear of the wing trailing-edge. The single 1,000 shp Lycoming T53-L-1 turboshaft engine drove two wing-mounted Hartzell three-blade wooden propellers of large diameter. Large endplates at the wingtips provided structural support for the flaps and confined the slipstream to the flap span for maximum efficiency. Conventional stick and rudder pedal controls were provided for the pilot to operate the rudder, elevator and variable-incidence tailplane, and the spoilers which were inset in the upper surface of each wing ahead of the flaps, taking the place of the usual ailerons. A universally jointed jet-deflection nozzle at the rear of the tailpipe from the engine was intended to ensure adequate control during the hovering flight mode.

As originally completed by Ryan in October 1957, the Vertiplane had a tailwheel-type undercarriage and a hood over the pilot's cockpit. Problems with the gearbox prevented taxiing trials from starting until 7 February 1958, and, after prolonged ground testing, including three months of tests in the full-scale low-speed wind tunnel of the NASA Ames Laboratory at Moffett Field, it made its first take-off as a conventional aeroplane on 29 December. Modifications made to the aircraft prior to the first flight, and as a result of the wind tunnel tests, were the substitution of a nosewheel undercarriage for the tailwheel type, new gearboxes, fitting of a deep ventral fin at the tail and of new retractable wing flaps. In the subsequent six-week test period the Vertiplane proved capable of near vertical take-offs at a ground speed of 40 km/h (25 mph), after a run of just 9 m (30 ft). It hovered at zero air speed at altitudes between 30 and 1,125 m (100 and 3,700 ft), and accomplished transitions from

**Ryan VZ-3RY Vertiplane**　(*Teledyne Ryan Aeronautical*)

hovering to forward flight. After making 21 successful flights and being delivered to NASA, the aircraft was virtually destroyed in an accident, when the left propeller did not change pitch during a landing sequence and the Vertiplane crash-landed.

NASA decided to have the Vertiplane rebuilt to continue the test programme, but in modified form. Changes included an ejection seat for pilot safety, lengthened forward fuselage, fitting of centre supports for the lower flaps, relocation of thrust line, a shallower ventral fin and a redesigned cockpit. In this form the Vertiplane flew on 4 December 1959, and thereafter underwent an extensive test programme.

In late 1961, after two years of research by Ryan and General Electric had proved the practicability of the 'fan-in-the-wing' principle for VTOL, the US Army Transportation Research Command awarded a contract for two XV-5A Vertifan aircraft to flight test the concept. General Electric was put in charge of contract manage-

ment and was responsible for the lift and propulsion systems. Ryan designed and built the aircraft.

Powered by two General Electric J85-GE-5 turbojet engines, each XV-5A had mid-positioned wings with single-slotted aluminium flaps and a trim tab in each aileron. A fan was located between the spars in each inner wing. The fuselage was of conventional structure but with a fan located in the nose. Longitudinally hinged air inlet doors above each wing fan and reverser doors under were fitted, while the nose fan had grille-type inlet doors. A variable incidence tailplane was mounted on top of the fin. Thrust spoilers aft of the tailpipes enabled the engines to be opened up to maximum power with the aircraft stationary, prior to the diverter valve being opened to release power to the fans for vertical lift.

The first XV-5A flew on 25 May 1964, and between that date and October 1966 the two aircraft accumulated a total of 138 flying hours in well

**Ryan XV-5A Vertifans**   *(Teledyne Ryan Aeronautical)*

over 300 flights in all modes of operation. However, the accident to an XV-5A in October marked the end of the XV-5A test programme, one aircraft having previously been lost in April 1965. The recently damaged XV-5A was taken away for rebuilding, emerging as the XV-5B. Modifications incorporated during rebuilding included a new wider track undercarriage, revised cockpit layout, and removal of the thrust spoiler mechanism. Preliminary flight tests of the XV-5B began on 24 June 1968 and the aircraft was subsequently delivered to NASA for further research.

In the 1950s Short Brothers and Harland developed the Short SC.1 research aircraft to Specification ER143, becoming the first fixed-wing VTOL aeroplane to be built in the United Kingdom. The first of two SC.1s flew initially on 2 April 1957, but as a conventional aeroplane. Of distinctive appearance, it had delta wings and a vertical tail surface only. The non-retractable undercarriage had pivoted main legs that could

be moved hydraulically through 15° fore-and-aft to enable the wheels to be positioned further aft of the centre of gravity during landing. Power was provided by five 966 kg (2,130 lb) thrust Rolls-Royce RB.108 turbojet engines, the four used for jet-lift mounted vertically in cross-wise pairs, each pair swinging on a transverse axis. In operation, after take-off the engines were inclined rearward to give added forward thrust; before vertical landing they could be directed forward to give a braking effect. A fifth engine exhausted horizontally at the tail for conventional forward thrust. All engines had a compressor bleed, supplying high-pressure air to a common duct which fed control nozzles at the wingtips, nose and tail.

Similar methods of achieving flight were used by several later aircraft, a few of which are described in this book. Interestingly, the Soviet Yakovlev Yak-36MP *Forger* VTOL combat aircraft currently in operational service uses similar principles. *Forger*'s primary propulsion unit is a single large turbojet engine, exhausting through

**Short SC.1** (*Air Portraits*)

a pair of vectoring side nozzles aft of the wings. Two smaller lift-jets are installed in tandem in the fuselage under a hinged louvred door. It is believed that these lift-jets are mounted at an angle in such a way that their thrust is exerted both upward and slightly forward. As the main vectored-thrust nozzles also turn up to 10° forward of vertical during take-off and landing, the total of four effluxes can be considered to form a V under the aircraft.

The second SC.1 began tethered vertical flight trials on 6 August 1958, using a specially-constructed gantry. A free vertical take-off was achieved from an open platform on 25 October. It was not until 20 July 1960 that the first SC.1 performed a vertical flight. Meanwhile the second SC.1 had demonstrated a complete transition from vertical to forward flight, and vice versa, on 6 April, thereafter transitions becoming routine. In May of the following year an SC.1 was flown to the *Salon de l'Aéronautique* in Paris, a stage of the flight from Manston in Kent to Coxyde in Belgium necessitating it to become the first jet-lift aircraft to fly the English Channel.

The second SC.1 was fitted with a Mk 3 auto-stabiliser, which controlled the emission of air from the nozzles at the wingtips, nose and tail. Unfortunately, on 2 October 1963 this aircraft crashed from low altitude, killing its pilot, after 81 flights with the Mk 3 auto-stabiliser had been made. The fault in the gyro system was quickly found and the aircraft rebuilt, this time carrying an instrument and automatic control system for development work relating to approach and landing in bad visibility. Tethered hovering resumed on 17 June 1966, and in 1967 both SC.1s were at the Royal Aircraft Establishment at Bedford for research into the landing characteristics of VTOL aircraft.

Similar in concept to the tilting-rotor aircraft were the tilt-wing types, a number of which enriched the aviation scene for nearly two decades from the latter 1950s. Though the promised production derivatives never got past the

**Vertol Model 76/VZ-2A    (*Boeing Vertol*)**

drawing board, the experimental prototypes provided one of the few realistic insights into a world of VTOL transports. Having said this, the first aircraft built to explore the possibilities of the then-unproved concept was little more than a flying test-bed, perhaps mindful of an aircraft built from a giant version of a child's metal construction kit.

This aircraft, the Vertol Model 76, was produced to US Office of Naval Research and US Army contract. The single 860 hp Lycoming YT53-L-1 turboshaft engine was geared to drive two three-blade rotor/propellers mounted on the wing. Two ducted fans mounted horizontally and vertically at the tail provided additional control and stability in vertical, hovering and low-speed flight. Unlike the Bell XV-3, on which only the rotor/propellers tilted during transitional flying, the complete wing and rotor/propellers tilted on the Model 76, during the downward conversion from vertical to horizontal flight the differential propeller collective-pitch system being phased out as a means of providing lateral control and conventional ailerons taking over.

With the military designation VZ-2A, the Model 76 began ground tests in April 1957, and on 13 August flew for the first time. On 23 July the following year it was announced that successful transitions from vertical to horizontal flight, and vice versa, had been completed. By May 1961, when flying was suspended temporarily while the wings were modified to improve stability and control during descent and the transmission uprated, the Model 76 had completed more than fifty hours of flying during 448 flights, including 239 partial and 34 full conversions.

For its X-18 tilt-wing aircraft, Hiller adopted the fuselage and other components of a Chase YC-122 transport. The high-set wing could vary in incidence from 4° normal to 90° at maximum tilt, 87° setting being used for vertical take-off. Pitch control changed from tailplane and elevators in horizontal flight to jet-diverter in vertical flight (using a standard 1,542 kg [3,400 lb] thrust Westinghouse J34 turbojet engine mounted in the rear fuselage, provided with an extended tailpipe and jet diverter). The two wing-mounted 5,850 eshp Allison T40-A-14 turboprop engines each drove

**Hiller X-18**

**LTV/Hiller/Ryan XC-142A**

Curtiss-Wright contra-rotating propellers of the type previously found on the tail-sitting fighters (see the second chapter). Maximum level speed was 402 km/h (250 mph).

The X-18 flew for the first time on 24 November 1959 as a conventional aeroplane. In more than 100 hours of ground and flight tests that followed it operated as a fixed-wing aircraft. Its wings were tilted progressively to an angle of attack of 50° before the flight programme was interrupted so that studies of downwash effects on the ground environment during hovering could be made, using a specially-prepared rig. Data from the X-18 programme was used with good effect in the development of the XC-142A.

Envisaged for the rapid deployment of approximately 32 fully-armed troops or for carrying 3,630 kg (8,000 lb) of equipment and supplies from assault ships or airfields into unprepared areas under all weather conditions, Chance Vought (later LTV), Hiller and Ryan developed jointly the experimental XC-142A VTOL tilt-wing transport for the US armed forces. LTV was prime contractor and the USAF assumed project management. Five flying prototypes and one static test airframe were ordered in 1962, one XC-142A making the first flight as a conventional aeroplane on 29 September 1964.

Each XC-142A was powered by four 3,080 shp General Electric T64-GE-1 turboprop engines, driving conventional propellers and a horizontally-mounted variable-pitch tail rotor. The wing was able to rotate through an angle of 100°, making possible hovering in a tailwind. In addition to vertical and horizontal flight, the XC-142A was capable of flying backward and of making 360° rotations in a hovering condition.

The first hovering flight of an XC-142A was performed on 29 December 1964; on 11 January the following year two full conversions were made. By February 1967 the five aircraft had flown 420 times to accumulate 350 hours in the air. Flying speeds had ranged from 56 km/h (35 mph) backward to 644 km/h (400 mph) in forward flight. The totals included one XC-142A making 44 short take-offs and landings (STOL) and six vertical take-offs and landings on the US aircraft carrier *Bennington* on 18 May 1966, while another aircraft was used extensively in air drop experiments, dropping dummy loads weighing up to 1,815 kg (4,000 lb).

In the same month as the XC-142A achieved its first hovering flight Canadair rolled out its CL-84, a tilt-wing V/STOL aircraft for close-support and utility transport roles. Designed on the same principles as the XC-142A, the Canadian aircraft

*Above:* **Canadair CL-84-1**

*Below:* **Canadair CL-84 during deck-landing experiments**

**Avro Avrocar**

was smaller and was powered by two 1,400 shp Lycoming T53 turboshaft engines. A horizontal contra-rotating tail rotor provided lift and pitch control during vertical and low-speed flight.

Preliminary research work had been funded by Canadair, the Canadian Defence Research Board and the Canadian Department of Defence Production, and the CL-84 made its first hovering flight on 7 May 1965. During the next three months low-speed and hovering tests were conducted and, following ground tests, a series of flights as a conventional aeroplane was made. On 17 January 1966 the first full transition was accomplished; during the next ten days twenty full conversions were performed. In 1966 the flight programme continued to develop fully the VTOL and STOL characteristics in preparation for operational evaluation by the military, the original fixed undercarriage also being replaced with a retractable gear. During this period the CL-84 performed three demonstrations of vertical hoisting in simulated air rescue from land and water, achieved 491 km/h (305 mph) in conven-

tional aeroplane mode, and carried out aerobatic 360° rolls in less than five seconds.

By mid-1967 the CL-84 had accumulated more than 122 hours in the air in 260 flights, during which 133 transitions had been made. This original aircraft was followed by three examples for evaluation by CAF (Canadian Armed Forces), military designated CX-84 but better remembered as CL-84-1s. The first flew on 19 February 1970. CAF evaluation included gun-firing trials in hovering, conventional and slow-speed tilt-wing flight; demonstrations from the Pentagon helicopter pad; and a series of take-offs and landings on board USS *Guam*. However, subsequent change of emphasis, from an updated CL-84-1 as a possible production model to an advanced CL-84 using two T64 turboprop engines, brought about the projected SCS CL-84, the letters SCS standing for Sea Control Ship. Designed to meet ship-based ASW and radar surveillance requirements, operating from a short deck, the SCS CL-84 was expected to have an all-up weight for VTOL operations of

**Fairey Rotodyne Y at the Westland Heliport pad**

13,154 kg (29,000 lb), compared with the AUW of 5,715 kg (12,600 lb) for the CL-84-1. In the event no CL-84 types became operational.

Although in no way connected with the CL-84, another Canadian VTOL aircraft of great interest was the Avro Avrocar, a genuine flying saucer of earthly origin! Developed for the US Department of Defense, the VZ-9V (to give it its US Army designation) was powered by three Continental J69 turbojet engines. These were used to drive the central fan which provided a peripheral air curtain and ground cushion for VTOL operation. In forward flight the saucer-shaped body of the aircraft developed aerodynamic lift and was intended to reach a maximum speed of 482 km/h (300 mph) at high altitude and a range of 1,600 km (1,000 miles).

The VZ-9V began tethered flight trials on 5 December 1959 and was subsequently moved to California for development testing. It was returned to Toronto for free forward flight trials, which began on 17 May 1961. Modified extensively during the development period, the con-

cept was quickly abandoned. Crew accommodation was interesting, with a member each side of the fan slightly forward of centre and under a bubble canopy.

As the tilt-wing concept for VTOL had several takers, so other techniques already mentioned could be found, often as not, on later aircraft. This is not to say that *all* aircraft with later first flight dates owed anything to previous types mentioned; some were developed in parallel, while others were much more advanced. A good example of the latter was the Fairey Rotodyne, a 40-passenger experimental VTOL transport convertiplane, first flown on 6 November 1957. Powered by two 3,000 ehp Napier Eland N.E.L.3 turboprop engines mounted under the wings, it was the culmination of experimentation with the Fairey Gyrodyne, which first flew in original form on 7 December 1947 as the first British convertiplane. In operation the Rotodyne's engines were coupled to auxiliary air compressors through a clutch. The compressors delivered air to pressure-jets at the rotor-tips, where fuel was

**Kamov Ka-22 Vintokryl**

burned to produce thrust rotation. It could be flown as a helicopter, or as an autogyro with engine power going only to the forward-facing propellers and the rotor autorotating. In practice, the tip-jets were used normally for take-off and landing, while for cruising flight the rotor autorotated. The first transition from vertical to horizontal flight was achieved on 10 April 1958, but the programme was abandoned in 1962 for economic reasons. The expected Rotodyne Z 54–70-passenger production version had been awaited eagerly by several airlines from around the world.

Another example of a later convertiplane was the huge Kamov Ka-22 Vintokryl, perhaps designed as an 80–100-passenger transport and making its first public appearance in the Soviet Union on 9 July 1961. The Vintokryl set up several world records for speed and payload from October 1961, the height record of 2,588 m (8,491 ft) and speed record in a straight line of 356.3 km/h (221.4 mph) still standing today.

However, the speed record in a 100 km closed circuit is held by the Rotodyne at 307.22 km/h (190.90 mph).

Similarly, the deflected slipstream technique used by the Ryan Vertiplane could be found on its contemporary, the Fairchild VZ-5FA, which first flew (tethered) on 18 November 1959. The tilting-rotor technique was adopted in modified form on the Curtiss-Wright X-100/X-19A aircraft of 1960–66, as the 'radial lift force' propeller concept. The Doak VZ-4DA convertiplane, first flown on 25 February 1958, used its single 840 shp Lycoming YT53 turboshaft engine to power tilting ducted propellers (or fans) at the wingtips to achieve vertical or horizontal flight, while ten years later the French Nord 500 research aircraft was built and flown to evaluate the tilting-duct concept, powered by two 317 shp Allison 250-C18 turboshaft engines driving five-blade ducted pusher propellers (or fans).

As mentioned in the second chapter, the current Rockwell International XFV-12A uses a

*Above:* **Fairchild VZ-5FA** (*Howard Levy*)

*Below:* **Curtiss-Wright X-100/X-19A**

**Above:** Doak VZ-4DA

**Below:** Nord 500

**Lockheed XV-4B Hummingbird II**    *(Lockheed-California)*

propulsion system very similar to that of the Lockheed XV-4A Hummingbird VTOL research aircraft of two decades before. The Hummingbird, powered by two 1,497 kg (3,300 lb) thrust Pratt & Whitney JT12A-3 (Mod) turbojet engines, first flew as a conventional aeroplane on 7 July 1962. Following tethered hovering flights, begun at the end of November 1962, it started a free hover-flight test programme in mid-1963, achieving a transition from vertical to horizontal mode on 8 November that year. After the crash of the first Hummingbird, the second was converted for direct jet-lift research as the XV-4B Hummingbird II, but crashed in 1969.

In its XV-4A form, the Hummingbird used both engines to provide thrust for VTOL and forward flight, by means of a system of diverter valves in the tailpipes. For take-off and landing, the valves diverted the entire efflux through 180° into a pair of ejector ducts. The efflux was discharged downwards from the ducts, through 20 transverse rows of multiple nozzles, into the two ejector chambers. In the top and bottom of the fuselage were bomb-bay type doors, which were opened for VTOL operations. When the high-velocity gases were ejected downward they drew with them a quantity of free air through the open doors. This air was accelerated by the hot gases issuing from the ejector nozzles and was expected to boost the vertical lift by about 40%. After vertical take-off the aircraft's nose was tilted down and it

began to move forward. One engine and then the other was switched to forward thrust, and the nose raised. Jet nozzles at the nose, tail and wingtips gave stability during vertical and slow-speed manoeuvres.

In 1960 the Piasecki Aircraft Corporation held no less than twelve US Army/US Navy contracts relating to vertical lift research, six of which were secret. At this time it was flying perhaps the strangest VTOL machine, part aircraft and part land vehicle. Known as the Piasecki Airgeep, it was developed under contract from the US Army Transportation Research Command. Intended for observation, liaison and other military duties, it had been designed to fly close to the ground, taking advantage of natural cover. However, it was in no way dependent on ground effect, and was fully capable of reaching an altitude of several thousand feet.

The original Model 59K Airgeep I was first flown on 12 October 1958, powered by two 180 hp Lycoming O-360-A2A piston engines. Later re-engined with Artouste IIB turboshafts, it accommodated the pilot and one passenger. It was followed by the improved Model 59H Airgeep II, given the military designation VZ-8P (B). The two horizontal opposite-rotating three-blade ducted rotors were driven by two 530 shp Turboméca Artouste IIC (modified) turboshaft engines. Its wheels could also be powered, allowing the Airgeep to be driven on land when

**Piasecki VZ-8P Airgeep I**

required or to be part flown and part driven for an extended range mission. Seating was provided for five persons, including pilot. Ground and flight tests of the Airgeep II in stripped configuration began in mid-1961; free flights started a year later. Interestingly, the Airgeep I had been fitted with a float undercarriage in 1960 for evaluation by the US Navy, while a civil version was also under consideration. A similar type of VTOL machine was also developed by Bensen as the Model B-10 Prop-Copter, first flown on 6 August 1958.

The final three types to be covered in this chapter were all of German origin – the Dornier Do 31-E, EWR VJ 101 and VFW-Fokker VAK 191B. All showed great promise, none more so than the Dornier. Two flying prototype Do 31-E V/STOL transports were constructed to a German Defence Ministry contract, with the assistance of Vereinigte Flugtechnische Werke and Hamburger Flugzeugbau. The Do 31-E1 first flew on

10 February 1967, the E3 on 14 July. Each aircraft had eight 2,000 kg (4,400 lb) thrust Rolls-Royce RB.162-4D turbojet engines for lift and two 7,000 kg (15,500 lb) thrust Pegasus 5-2 vectored-thrust propulsion engines for lift/cruise flight. For vertical take-off, the nozzles of the main underwing engines were swivelled downward to combine power with the four lift-jets in each wing-tip pod, Within twenty seconds of take-off the aircraft could be flying at a level speed of 360 km/h (224 mph), the nozzles having rotated back to an aft-facing position and the eight lift-jets then switched off. Maximum cruising speed was 650 km/h (400 mph). The location of the lift-jets on the wingtips ensured effective compensation of roll if a main engine failed during VTOL. For pitch control, high-pressure bleed air from the lift-jets was ducted to nozzles at the stern of the aircraft. Roll control was achieved by thrust modulation of the lift-jets, and yaw control by differential tilting of the lift engine nozzles. Rate

of climb and descent were set with the output of the Pegasus engines.

Prior to construction of the Do 31s, Dornier had built the Control Systems Test Rig. It was a simple cruciform open girder structure, powered by four Rolls-Royce RB.108 lift-jets. Completed in 1964, it was used for hundreds of tests both on the ground and in the air. A second hovering rig, known as the Big Rig, was closer to a Do 31 proper but had six lift-jets, a partially-covered fuselage and a scant vertical tail. First hovered on 7 February 1967, it was incapable of wing-borne flying and was subsequently used in the further development of the hover control systems and to evaluate take-off and landing techniques. The second Do 31-E (E3) performed the first transition from vertical take-off to horizontal flight, on 16 December 1967, and the first transition from horizontal flight to vertical landing, on 21 December. By mid-1969 110 take-offs had been made, including many transitions, and the

aircraft was studied by a team of engineers and scientists from NASA. The test programme continued until the spring of 1970. The projected Do 131 operational V/STOL transport aircraft differed considerably from the experimental Do 31-Es, although probably accommodating a similar load of vehicles/freight, 36 troops or 24 stretchers. The two main engines were to have been RB.168-25-38 turbofans, while fourteen RB.162-81 lift-jets were to be mounted in two pods at about mid-span. The lift-jet pods were designed as detachable units, allowing the aircraft to be flown in conventional mode with optional fuel tanks in place of the pods. The Do 131 project was subsequently abandoned, as was the later Do 231, considered in both military and 100-passenger civil versions.

The EWR VJ 101 was designed to provide data to assist the development of a projected Mach 2 VTOL fighter. Two aircraft were built, as X-1 and X-2, X-2 taking over the development programme

**Bensen Model B-10 Prop-Copter**

**Dornier Do 31-E**    (*Dornier*)

**EWR VJ 101 X-1**

**VFW-Fokker VAK 191B**

after the first had crashed on 4 September 1964, but not before X-1 had made a free hovering flight on 10 April 1963, a transition on 20 September 1963, and exceeded Mach 1 in level flight. Both aircraft were powered by six Rolls-Royce RB.145 turbojet engines, two vertically-mounted in the fuselage bay and two in each swivelling wingtip pod. The wingtip engines of the second VJ 101C had afterburning to make possible speeds of well over Mach 1. The triangulated lift forces from the three sets of engines made possible control of the aircraft in VTOL flight by thrust modulation, so dispensing with the need for 'puffer-pipes'. The first full transition was performed on 22 October 1965.

The last of the three, the VFW-Fokker VAK 191B, was an experimental single-seat tactical strike and reconnaissance fighter with subsonic performance. It was a development of the earlier Focke-Wulf Fw 1262, for which a design study had been produced, and was initially managed by the German and Italian Defence Ministries under a 1964 agreement. In 1968 the Italian government pulled out of the project. Aimed at eventually producing a V/STOL aircraft to replace the Fiat G91s in German service, three VAK 191B prototypes were constructed, the first

flying in September 1971 after hovering trials. On 26 October 1972 the first vertical-to-horizontal transition was performed successfully, but the programme was eventually abandoned. Power for each aircraft was provided by two 2,530 kg (5,577 lb) thrust Rolls-Royce RB.162-81 lift-jets mounted vertically in the fuselage, and one 4,603 kg (10,150 lb) thrust Rolls-Royce/MTU RB.193-12 vectored-thrust turbojet for forward propulsion. The forward exhaust doors of both lift-jets extended to act as airbrakes, while stabilisation was achieved by 'puffer-jets' at the nose, tail and wingtips.

Experience of vertical take-off has never been available to the general public in the forms mentioned here, so what of the future? With even the largest aircraft manufacturers having to cut down production rate because of falling orders, it seems ever more likely that the helicopter will be the only civil VTOL aircraft available in the 1980s and probably well beyond. Finance for the development of more adventurous VTOL aircraft for non-military use will not be made available in these circumstances. More advanced versions of the military Harrier and Yak-36 will be forthcoming, but hopefully will never be required to see action.

# 5. A New Approach

*Above:* **Cornu helicopter**          *Below:* **Breguet brothers' helicopter**

Historians record that the first man-carrying helicopters to fly appeared in 1907, constructed by the Breguet brothers and Paul Cornu. Of little practical use, they echoed Wilbur Wright's words: 'Like all novices we began with the helicopter . . . but soon saw that it had no future and dropped it. The helicopter does with great labour only what the hydrogen balloon does without labour . . . .' Some would-be fliers agreed with this sentiment but still thought they could improve upon the more accepted fixed wings and propeller layout. The result was the ornithopter, an aircraft with flapping or oscillating wings but which did not rotate. Most tried to emulate the wing movements of the bird. Some, like that built by H.J. Passat in 1910, attempting also to look like one.

The helicopter went through a void period up to the mid-1930s. Even the Russian-born Igor Sikorsky, later famed for making the first successful free helicopter flight outside Germany (on 13 May 1940) in his VS-300 and progenitor of today's Sikorsky helicopters, shifted to fixed-wing designs after his failures around 1910. This void was partially filled by the gyroplane or auto-gyro, an aircraft with a free-turning rotor and a conventional tractor- or pusher-mounted engine and propeller to drive the craft forward. At speed the free-turning (or autorotating) rotor gave sufficient lift to keep the aircraft in the air, often supplemented by stub wings. The first successful model was the C4 of 1923, designed by the Spaniard Juan de la Cierva. His C6D was the first two-seater, while the C8L Mk II became the first

**Passat ornithopter**    (*Flight*)                **The first Cierva autogiro, a failure**    (*Flight*)

**Cierva C8**

rotating-wing aircraft to fly across the English Channel, on 18 September 1928.

Up to 1944, when the Sikorsky R-4 became the first helicopter in the world to go into series production proper for the US and British forces for observation and training roles, Germany took most honours. The Focke-Wulf Fw 61 was the world's first successful helicopter, first flying on 26 June 1936. In 1937 it covered more than 122 km (76 miles) in a closed circuit, and in the following year demonstrated forward, backward and sideways flight at the hands of the famous German woman test pilot Hanna Reitsch. While an important design, it had little lifting capacity and therefore remained a prototype. But Germany preparing for war had many far reaching ideas, including a place for a transport helicopter. With the basic layout of the Fw 61, the Focke-Achgelis Fa 266 Hornisse appeared in 1939 as a six-seater, ostensibly for commercial use by Luft-Hansa. It made its first free flight in August of the following year under the new designation Fa 223 Drache, by then a full military prototype. With roles including transport and anti-submarine patrol within its capability, thirty pre-production Draches were ordered. Successful Allied bombing prevented all but a few being built, the factory moving from Bremen to

**Focke-Wulf Fw 61**

Laupheim and then Berlin to escape destruction. In the event only three served with Lufttransportstaffel 40. Interestingly, film survived the war of Fa 223s undergoing flying-crane trials. An actual flying crane development of the Fa 223 was designed as the Fa 284, but was never built.

Germany also claimed the first jet-driven helicopter in the form of the Doblhoff/WNF 342, which used compressed air and fuel fed through the hollow rotor blades to power its three rotor tip-jets. The first 342 flew initially in early 1943. Meanwhile, another designer had been hard at work attempting to fulfil a German Navy requirement. Anton Flettner began experimenting in the field of helicopters in 1930, and eight years later received a contract for Fl 265 prototypes for evaluation by the Navy. Unlike his earlier designs the Fl 265 had intermeshing contrarotating rotors, powered by a single 150 hp

Siemens Sh 14A engine in the nose of the fuselage. An enclosed cabin was provided for the pilot. The first Fl 265 flew in mid-1939, but the type remained a prototype following the design of the improved Fl 282 Kolibri. As well as having the advantage of being a two-seater, forward view was improved by the positioning of the engine aft of the crew. Flying began in 1941 and sea trials started the following year. A large number of pre-production Fl 282s were ordered, some finding their way into active service as reconnaissance aircraft on convoy duty and as transports. Capable of operating from ships and shore, even in poor weather conditions, no less than 1,000 were ordered in 1944, only a handful of which were completed.

Another project worthy of mention was the Focke-Wulf Triebflügel. Basically a tail-sitting single-seat fighter, it was designed to have three

**Flettner Fl 265**    (*Real Photographs*)

**Flettner Fl 282 Kolibri**    (*Imperial War Museum*)

**McDonnell XHJD-1 Whirlaway stands by the tiny XH-20 Little Henry**   (*McDonnell Douglas*)

wings to rotate around the upper fuselage by the power of tip-mounted ramjet engines. This aircraft was never built.

After the war it was the American Bell and Sikorsky companies that carved the biggest impressions on the helicopter scene, while it took the Korean war of the early 1950s to set the seal on widespread use of helicopters in war, a foretaste of the massive operations in the later Vietnam conflict.

For the purposes of this book, the first post-war fantastic flying machine in the helicopter field was the McDonnell XHJD-1 Whirlaway, the world's first twin-engined helicopter. Only one example was built to US Navy contract, its design owing something to the twin-rotor Platt-Le Page XR-1 of wartime origin, which was successfully tested by the Rotary Wing Branch of the Air Technical Service Command, US Army. Powered by a single Pratt & Whitney R-985-AN1 engine and accommodating a crew of two in tandem in the glazed nose, the XR-1 and the more heavily glazed XR-1A were viewed by McDonnell personnel in 1943. McDonnell's own Whirlaway was ordered on 15 May 1944 and first flew on 27 April 1946. Over the next 2½ years more than 250

hours of flying were accumulated, but no production orders followed.

Among the helicopters produced by McDonnell during the 1940s and 1950s were two diminutive but nevertheless very interesting experimental types, the XH-20 Little Henry and Model 120. Little Henry was developed to use rotortip-mounted ramjet combustors, fuelled by propane gas for ground and tethered hovering tests and subsequently by gasoline. Two examples were constructed to Air Force contract, the first making a free flight on 20 August 1947. The test programme continued until 1951, but the high noise level combined with high fuel consumption prevented any other examples being built. A civil utility/agricultural version was also planned as the Model 79 Big Henry.

Although Little Henry's ramjets had not proved completely successful, the rotortip-driven helicopter offered several advantages over conventionally-driven types. Advantages included no engine parts, gear systems or transmission to go wrong and simplified cyclic control. Whilst having to forgo some of these advantages, later McDonnell helicopter/convertiplane designs incorporated rotor pres-

**McDonnell Model 120**

**Hughes XH-17**  (*Hughes Helicopters*)

sure jets which allowed simplified transmissions, etc. Examples were the XHRH-1 30-troop experimental compound helicopter for assault duties with the USMC (mock-up only, 1951–53), XV-1 (covered in the fourth chapter), XHCH-1 non-compound version of the XHRH-1 for rapid unloading and transport duties in forward areas with the US Navy (mock-up only, 1953–59), Model 113 light or medium cargo/troop transport or rescue helicopter with pressure jet or shaft-driven rotor, and the Model 120. The latter was a lightweight helicopter, designed as a private venture for flying crane duties with the US Army. Powered by three AiResearch GCT-85-125 turbo-compressors to supply compressed air to pressure-jets at the tips of the rotor, it was claimed that any engine could be replaced in five minutes without tools. The fuselage was extremely simple to minimise maintenance and to facilitate cargo loading. Cargo was carried suspended from a pilot-controlled cargo hook located below the rotor. Alternatively, up to 12 people could be accommodated on 'toboggan seats' in a detachable pod. Publicised as the first helicopter capable of lifting a load greater than its own weight, it had an estimated maximum speed of 222 km/h (138 mph). First flight was made on 13 November 1957, but lack of further interest by the Army caused the development programme to end in early 1959. The US Navy then became interested and evaluated the Model 120, but again no orders followed and the helicopter was abandoned for good in 1960.

Whereas the Model 120 had been developed as a small flying crane, the earlier Hughes XH-17 flying crane testbed had a gross weight of 19,960 kg (43,000 lb), 2½-times greater than any other contemporary helicopter. Developed from the Kellett XH-17 Flying Crane to a 1948 USAF contract, it first flew on 23 October 1952 and completed successfully its flight test programme the following year. Powered by two specially-modified General Electric GE 5500 turbojet engines, which supplied gas pressure through ducts leading up the rotor shaft and out of the tips of the 37.62 m (130 ft) diameter rotor, its flight control system had dual hydraulics, similar to the type fitted to the H-4 Hercules flying-boat. The long legs enabled the helicopter to manoeuvre over bulky cargoes prior to take-off – including heavy artillery, bridge sections or portable build-

**Hughes XV-9A**

ings – and so was the forerunner of today's heavy-lift types. Success with the XH-17 resulted in a follow-on order, under the designation XH-28. Designed to be the first helicopter capable of taking-off with a gross weight twice that of its empty weight, the XH-28's maximum take-off weight would have been about 47,627 kg (105,000 lb). A full-size mock-up was constructed but the project was abandoned as the Korean war forced spending in other directions.

One result of the XH-28 programme was that Hughes retained engineers to improve upon the pressure-jet propulsion system, culminating in development of the hot-cycle system. In this system the turbine efflux from two General Electric YT64-GE-6 gas generators was ducted through the rotor hub and 16.76 m (55 ft) diameter rotor to blade cascades. The gas temperature of approximately 649°C (1,200°F) made necessary the use of Rene 41 high-temperature steel for the internal duct structure between the spars. The expected improved propulsion efficiency meant lower fuel consumption than the pressure-jet sys-

**Fiat Model 7002**

tem. Hughes completed 60 hours of test running with a prototype hot-cycle rotor on a ground rig in 1962. The complete propulsion module comprising power plant, stub wing and rotor assembly was tested for 15 hours in early 1964 before being installed on a fuselage. The actual XV-9A research aircraft airframe was built of parts from other aircraft to save costs and time. Flight tests began on 5 November 1964 and ended in August the following year. The system showed a high degree of reliability. However, it was clear that the aircraft itself had poor handling characteristics, bad stability about all axes and poor control, while the system dictated increased weight and complexity of construction because of the high duct temperatures.

In Italy Fiat produced the Model 7002, which first flew on 26 January 1961. Accommodating seven persons or a crew of two and freight, the helicopter's main rotor was of the 'cold-jet' type. In this the rotor was turned by ejecting compressed air, without any form of combustion, from nozzles at the tips. Meanwhile, in Britain the Westland company had fitted a Sikorsky S-56 transmission and rotor to a new airframe to pro-

duce the Westminster flying crane, powered by two 3,150 shp Napier Eland E.229A turboshaft engines. Two prototypes only were built, the first flying initially on 15 June 1958 with little skin covering on the fuselage. This helicopter was later fully skinned and given a six-blade main rotor to investigate blade-stall problems at certain speeds.

Back in the USA, on 2 November 1962 Lockheed first flew its XH-51A high-performance helicopter. Its main power plant was a 500 shp Pratt & Whitney (Canada) T74 turboshaft engine, driving a four-blade rigid main rotor. This form of rotor was pioneered on the Lockheed CL-475 flying testbed helicopter, and was claimed to have inherent stability without artificial stabilisation, high manoeuvrability, extremely wide usable CG range, low vibration and ease of control. It had cantilevered blades, with freedom in the feathering axis only. Two XH-51A helicopters were completed to US Army/Navy contract, and these were eventually tested in three forms, as the XH-51A, XH-51A Compound and XH-51N. Of these, the Compound, which had a Pratt & Whitney J60-P-2 auxiliary turbojet engine and short-

**Westland Westminster**  (*Westland Aircraft*)
**Lockheed XH-51A Compound**  (*Lockheed-California*)

**Lockheed AH-56A Cheyenne**

span wings, established an unofficial record for rotating-wing aircraft of 487 km/h (302.6 mph) in June 1967, so becoming the first rotary-wing aircraft to exceed 300 mph. The XH-51N was similar to the 'A' but had a three-blade rotor and could seat five. A five-seat utility helicopter evolved from the XH-51A was subsequently produced by Lockheed as the Model 286, but little came of this.

Following the outstanding success of the Bell HueyCobra in the new high-speed close-support helicopter role, the US Army quickly decided to encourage development of second-generation types. After a hotly-contested design competition, Lockheed received a contract in 1966 for engineering development of an Advanced Aerial Fire Support System (AAFSS) helicopter. The contract included funds for the construction of ten prototypes designated AH-56A Cheyenne. The first flight of a prototype proper was made on 21 September 1967, and on 7 January 1968 the

US Department of Defense gave approval for the production of 375 AH-56As. However, this order was cancelled in the spring of 1969 and further development of the helicopter was abandoned.

Powered by one 3,435 shp General Electric T64-GE-16 turboshaft engine, which powered the rotors and a pusher propeller, the AH-56A had a maximum speed of 393 km/h (244 mph). Armament included a 40 mm grenade launcher or a 7.62 mm Minigun in the nose turret, a 30 mm cannon in a swivelling belly turret, and rockets or anti-tank missiles under the stub wings and fuselage. Interestingly, a second generation attack helicopter had still not entered service at the time of writing in early 1981, although the Hughes AH-64 is expected to become operational in about 1984.

On 27 May 1970 Boeing Vertol first flew its Model 347 research helicopter. Basically a modified CH-47A with four-blade rotors, a stretched fuselage, increased aft pylon height, retractable landing gear, uprated engines and transmission, advanced flight controls, improved cockpit, self-contained navigation system, vibration suppression and structural tuning, it was used in a two-phase flight test programme. Phase I covered tests as a pure helicopter, in which it demonstrated a power-limited maximum speed of 325 km/h (202 mph), low noise and vibration levels, and superior stability and control characteristics in manual and automatic flight path control modes. Phase II tests began in December 1971 with the helicopter fitted with wings capable of being rotated from a 10° nose-down attitude in autorotation to an 85° nose-up attitude in hover. This phase was aimed at assessing the influence of the wings on manoeuvrability. The helicopter was later given a retractable under-fuselage capsule, to evaluate the load-controlling crewman's station, and functions, for the projected XCH-62 heavy lift helicopter.

In contrast to the large Boeing Vertol, three one-man helicopters of interest appeared in the early 1970s. Probably the most important was the Aerospace General Mini-Copter, developed eventually into four separate forms. As originally conceived, and later known as Configuration 1, it was a strap-on helicopter to be air-dropped in a standard US Navy aerial delivery container to a pilot who had been forced down behind enemy lines or in terrain unsuited to conventional rescue craft. The helicopter comprised a control/rotor unit and fuel tanks which the pilot could strap onto his back. Two 19 kg (42 lb) thrust Aerospace General rocket motors were mounted on the tips of the rotor blades for power. Configuration 1 was first flown on 31 March 1973. Configuration 2 was similar except that the basic unit was mounted on a steel-tube structure with skid undercarriage to provide a seat for the pilot, while Configuration 3 had extended range by

**Boeing Vertol Model 347**    (*Boeing Vertol*)

*Above:* **Aerospace General Mini-Copter Configuration 1**          *Below:* **Gluhareff Helicopters MEG-3X**

**Gluhareff Helicopters MEG-2X**

virtue of its pusher-mounted 90 hp McCulloch engine, enabling operation as an autogyro. A civil version of the last configuration was also conceived as the MC-8 Mini-Copter.

Helicopters similar to Configuration 1 and 2 were also built in Denmark by engineer and amateur constructor W. Vincent Seremet, his W.S.8 of 1976 using a 35 hp Kiekhaefer piston engine to power the rotor. This was a modification of the earlier W.S.4A, itself originating as a strap-on type. Unlike the American Mini-Copter, the W.S.8 used a tripod undercarriage.

The third type was produced by Gluhareff

Helicopters, an American company that also flew the MEG-3X jet-rotor flying platform under US Navy contract. Its MEG-2X strap-on helicopter was powered by Gluhareff G8-2-15 tip-jets with a maximum endurance of 12 minutes. Maximum forward speed was estimated at 88.5 km/h (55 mph) and hovering ceiling at 1,370 m (4,500 ft), low figures when compared to the Aerospace General Mini-Copter's maximum speed of 177 km/h (110 mph) and hovering ceiling of more than 6,100 m (20,000 ft). Unlike the Mini-Copter and W.S.8, the MEG-2X carried an anti-torque fin instead of a tail rotor.

**Mil V-12 (Mi-12)**

Equally suited to the seventh chapter, the Soviet Mil V-12 (Mi-12) was (and remains) the largest helicopter ever built, intended to carry payloads compatible with those of the Antonov An-22 fixed-wing heavy transport. Powered by four 6,500 shp Soloviev D-25VF turboshaft engines, driving two five-blade rotors on outriggers, it could carry a 30,000 kg (66,000 lb) payload as normal, perhaps made up of fifty troops (or members of a work crew) and freight which could include large vehicles. Known to NATO as *Homer*, it is believed to have first flown in 1969 and went on to set a number of payload-to-height records. The first prototype was reported to have crashed that year, but further prototypes followed. However, it appears that this helicopter remained a prototype, while more recently a new heavy-lift helicopter of Boeing 727 size has been developed by Mil, known to NATO as *Halo*.

**Edgley EA7 Optica**   (*Austin J. Brown*)

The last aircraft to be covered in this chapter is not a helicopter but a three-seat, slow-flying observation aeroplane of British origin, known as the Edgley EA7 Optica. Powered by a ducted propulsor unit, with the Avco Lycoming piston engine and fan forming a power pod separate from the main shroud, it is intended to undertake many roles currently performed by expensive-to-operate helicopters at considerably lower overall cost. These roles could include pipeline and powerline inspection, forestry and coastal patrol, police traffic patrol, frontier patrol, aerial photography, TV and press reporting and touring. The cabin configuration is based upon that of an insect's eye, to give the best possible all-round view from a fixed-wing aircraft. It has STOL capability from both hard and soft strips and a range of 1,000 km (620 miles) at 65% power cruising speed. Loiter speed is 92 km/h (57 mph). Low volume production is expected to begin shortly.

# 6. Glassfibre and foam

Some of the most interesting aircraft have derived from an enormous number of worldwide aviation enthusiasts who are linked by the collective name of homebuilders. This word is self-explanatory, separating their activities from those of the professional aircraft constructors and companies that design and build for the large scale requirements of civil and military operations. We must not forget, however, that all of aviation's pioneers were homebuilders, and that prior to the beginning of World War I, a high proportion of all aircraft then flying had been originated as rule-of-thumb one-offs. Further, such is the importance of homebuilt aircraft that *Jane's All the World's Aircraft* contains a section devoted exclusively to this grouping, while a number of companies are included as 'homebuilders' as they prepare and manufacture plans and kits of parts of their respective aircraft for sale to amateur constructors.

The advent of World War I resulted in large-scale production of military aeroplanes. The earliest of these were little more than adaptations of aircraft in use before hostilities began, but the impetus of conflict brought enhanced capability and complexity. Professional constructors also learned how to build in large numbers, and in the immediate post-war years there were available vast numbers of unwanted ex-military aircraft at almost give-away prices. These could be acquired and used by demobbed airmen or by those with an ambition to learn to fly one of these new-fangled machines. It was a time when comparatively few of the world's population were airminded, and because of the surplus aircraft available there was little incentive for individual innovation. It needed the highly publicised and exciting continent-linking activities of the between-wars trail-blazing pilots to make people realise that aviation could be of benefit to the ordinary man and woman.

Then came World War II, when hundreds of thousands of those men and women, then serving in the armed forces of combatant nations, discovered that they were being moved around the world speedily, safely (as war allowed), but not necessarily comfortably, in military transports. The advantages for peacetime travel were apparent, and the enormous growth in air travel began quickly when the conflict ended.

Not only had vast numbers of people flown in the services, and wanted to enjoy the delights of peacetime aviation, but a whole generation of young men had also acquired new and advanced technical competence. It was from these men, to a large extent, that the real homebuilding movement was generated. The sheer cost of acquiring a new factory-built lightplane was, in any case, far beyond the reach of most enthusiasts, who needed also to finance homes, families, and the world-invading motor

**Santos-Dumont Demoiselle**

car. And there were very few ex-military aircraft up for grabs this time. But, with a little skill and ingenuity an aircraft could be built bit by bit, as finances allowed, with the ultimate goal of becoming airborne as a constant spur to progress.

The homebuilding movement of the 1980s includes men and women from every part of the world. Of this number, of course, comparatively few have the capability to design a machine which is aerodynamically suitable to fly efficiently, and has the structural integrity to withstand hard use and often, in the early stages of flight familiarisation, rough treatment. As a result, many designs have been originated by those with experience gained in the course of earning their living within the aerospace industry. Following the evolution of an original design, and the construction of a prototype, plans have often been made available at moderate cost so that enthusiastic handymen can create a similar aircraft. In some cases the task has been made easier with availability of kits of parts or indi-

vidual difficult-to-fabricate components being offered for sale. A few of the most popular homebuilts have captured a worldwide market, with many thousands of sets of plans sold. Others have gone into limited production in foreign countries for civil and military use, although remaining homebuilts elsewhere.

This aspect of the homebuilt movement is not new. As long ago as 1907 the little Brazilian Alberto Santos-Dumont (see the first chapter) had built the first of a family of very small aircraft which acquired the overall name of Demoiselle (Dragonfly). That of 1909 was a graceful monoplane constructed largely of bamboo and wire, the high-mounted wing covered with silk and supporting the 25 hp water-cooled petrol engine. Its design was available freely to anyone who wished to try and emulate Santos-Dumont's achievements, but to be successful they needed also to have his diminutive, lightweight physique. If only a few pounds heavier, the total load would be too much for the little aeroplane to lift

**H.M. 14 Pou du Ciel**

into the air. Also would-be pilots had to tolerate a high landing speed while seated just inches from the ground.

Santos-Dumont was, therefore, the first of the homebuilders in the modern sense, creating a design that was available for others to copy. But while the Demoiselle was of classic configuration, that of the French-designed Pou du Ciel (Flying Flea or Sky Louse) was far more revolutionary. In the 1930s Henri Mignet, who for some years had been involved in the design and construction of lightplanes, finalised his ideas on a new easy to build and easy to fly aircraft. Powered by a 17 hp engine in its 1935 form, this small monoplane dispensed with both ailerons and elevators. A wide-chord short-span wing was hinged to provide variable incidence, actuated by fore and aft movements of the control column. This wing, and the large tailplane which was mounted quite close to and only slightly lower than the main wing, both had considerable dihedral to provide lateral stability. Directional control came from the rudder, actuated by sideways movement of the control column, so that the

novice had only a single flight control to master. Henri Mignet produced a manual giving full building instructions, available to anyone intending to produce an aircraft for his or her own use. Unfortunately, there was an inadequate degree of control in pitch, resulting in several fatal accidents, and a design that had seemed to offer an 'everyman's' flying-machine was to become just another page in aviation's inspiring history.

No reference to the Flying Flea would be complete without mention of the first Flying Flea rally, organised by an Englishman in Essex in the mid-1930s. Aircraft were trailered in to the field or carried on carts and lorries by their proud owners in preparation for a grand 'fly-in'. With Flying Fleas screeching up and down the field it soon became obvious that none would leave the ground. Then, unexpectedly, one lifted off, only to finish in a tree. On closer inspection it was found that the aircraft had clipped wings for ground training and should have been incapable of flight. More astonishing was that at the controls was a small boy, somewhat shocked by his experience. So much for the original Flying Flea,

**Breezy RLU-1** *(J. M. G. Gradidge)*

but today several aircraft based on the same concept fly successfully.

The true homebuilt age blossomed in the USA in the years following World War II, activities aided by the Experimental Aircraft Association (EAA) which was founded to advise would-be homebuilders, and later to help them gain new skills in the art of designing and building. Not surprisingly, their early activities followed conventional design, with new biplanes and monoplanes being created, built and flown in large numbers. During the 1950s and 1960s their ranks grew, but with a growing shortage of hydrocarbon fuels and a genuine attempt to produce the simplest aircraft possible, a new generation of aircraft took to the skies in the 1970s, as these enthusiasts looked to new materials and new configurations to provide light weight and economical performance. It is from this area of development that some of the most fantastic new aircraft have emerged.

One of the earliest was the RLU-1 Breezy, which flew for the first time on 7 August 1964. RLU derives from the surnames of the three pro-fessional pilots who dreamed up the Breezy (Roloff, Liposky and Unger), their aim being to create a lightweight structure that would give good performance on the power of a 90 hp piston engine. The fuselage comprises an uncovered triangular-section welded steel tube structure. Above it is strut-mounted a standard Piper PA-12 lightplane wing, the struts serving also to mount the engine which drives a pusher propeller. A conventional tail unit is at the aft end of the fuselage, tricycle undercarriage beneath the fuselage, and pilot and passenger accommodated on fully exposed seats forward of the wing, so that the name Breezy has real meaning. Maximum take-off weight is 544 kg (1,200 lb) and normal cruising speed 121 km/h (75 mph). By mid-1980 more than 700 sets of plans to construct the Breezy had been sold, with examples flying in Australia, Canada, South Africa, Switzerland and the USA.

Similar in overall configuration to the Breezy, but using very different constructional techniques, is the very popular Hovey Whing Ding II biplane. In this case the forward fuselage is a

**Hovey Whing Ding II**

plywood box structure, filled with urethane foam to give it rigidity, and the tailboom an aluminium tube reinforced with epoxy bonded light alloy sheet at the forward end. Wing and tail surfaces are fabric covered. The 14 hp McCulloch go-kart engine mounted similarly to that of the Breezy drives a pusher propeller, and a single exposed seat forward of the wings is provided for the pilot. In this aircraft the empty weight (including fuel) is only 55.5 kg (123 lb), showing what can be done by utilising new structural materials and techniques, and its economic cruising speed is 64.5 km/h (40 mph).

Bob Hovey's Whing Ding II was first flown in February 1971, and since that time more than 7,000 sets of plans have been sold to amateur constructors, giving some indication of the interest in this fascinating hobby. Just over a year after that flight, one of the most beautiful homebuilts currently available in plan and material kit form for construction by amateur builders flew for the first time. Named the Larkin KC-3 Skylark, it is a two-seater of light alloy and glass-

fibre construction, possessing a cruising speed of 169 km/h (105 mph). In the same year the first of Bert Rutan's family of unmistakable canards took to the air, as the VariViggen. Its design had started nine years earlier, the aim being to build an aircraft which could be flown safely by a homebuilder after he received the minimum amount of instruction to fly solo. Five of those nine years were spent in refining the design and carrying out tests with a one-fifth scale model which was 'flown' on a special rig mounted on the roof of a motor car. Bert Rutan had finalised a spin-proof configuration before starting construction of the prototype in 1968. It has low-mounted wings of cropped delta configuration at the rear of a fuselage which provides comfortable accommodation for two people seated in tandem. Ailerons are incorporated in the trailing-edge of the wings, between each fin and rudder and wingtip. Slotted flap-type elevators form part of the canard foreplane structure, carried high on the nose and forward of the windscreen. Power is provided by a 150 hp piston engine mounted

**Larkin KC-3 Skylark**

**Rutan VariEzes** (*Don Dwiggins*)

**Above:** Birdman TL-1A          **Below:** Sawyer Skyjacker II

within the rear fuselage, and driving a pusher propeller. Maximum take-off weight is 771 kg (1,700 lb), and it has an economic cruising speed of 201 km/h (125 mph). Interestingly, a twin Microturbo turbojet-engined adaptation of the VariViggen has been built in France as the Chagnes Microstar. Maximum speed has been stated at 400 km/h (248 mph), compared with 262 km/h (163 mph) for the standard aircraft.

Very different to the Whing Ding, the VariViggen was to demonstrate in its original form the realisation of its designer's dreams, able to climb, cruise, glide, turn and land with continuous full aft stick, without the least sign of any vicious tendencies. The VariViggen was followed by the easier-to-build VariEze of somewhat similar configuration, using a large amount of unidirectional glassfibre with rigid foam as a core material. The most noticeable changes are substitution of a more-conventional but rear-mounted swept wing, with an above-wing 'winglet' at each tip incorporating a rudder; and with the retractable tricycle undercarriage replaced by non-retractable main units and a manually-retracted nosewheel. Power is reduced to 100 hp, allowing an empty weight of only 254 kg (560 lb), while maximum take-off weight is 476 kg (1,050 lb) and economic cruising speed 265 km/h (165 mph). By mid-1980 approximately 2,000 VariEzes were being constructed, with 220 already flying, while about 900 sets of plans for the VariViggen had been sold. Also, a four-seat lightplane of twin-engined 'push and pull' type has been flown as the Rutan Defiant, similar in shape to the VariEze.

A generally similar aircraft to the VariEze is the longer-range Long-EZ, first flown on 12 June 1979. Of slightly larger dimensions and carrying more than double the quantity of fuel, it has a maximum take-off weight of 601 kg (1,325 lb) and an economic cruising speed of 232 km/h (144 mph). Flying this aircraft during 15–16 December 1979, Dick Rutan established a new world closed-circuit distance record in FAI Class C1b of 7,725.3 km (4,800.3 miles), proving emphatically that homebuilt aircraft had reached an unprecedented plateau of capability. This point can be underlined by another homebuilt aircraft, the Red Baron F-104RB Starfighter. The fastest and undoubtedly most complicated homebuilt ever flown, it was basically a modified

Lockheed F-104 Starfighter jet fighter, built over many years from gathered components by its pilot Darryl Greenamyer. On 24 October 1977 this aircraft, flying at Mud Lake, Nevada, set an absolute world speed record over a 3 km course at restricted (low) altitude of 1,590.45 km/h (988.26 mph), in Class C, group III, thus ranking with the fastest military aircraft flown by the US and Soviet air forces on record attempts. Unfortunately the F-104RB was lost in an accident just before an attempt was to be made on the existing altitude record held by the Soviet Union.

The year 1975 was one in which a number of interesting new designs were flown for the first time, and taking them alphabetically we begin with the Birdman TL-1 which, in its original prototype form, was the world's lightest powered aircraft, weighing in at just 45 kg (100 lb). Since it first flew, on 25 January, it has been improved to its present TL-1A standard. This consists of a cantilever monoplane wing of wood and expanded foam with Monokote covering, a fuselage of composite light alloy and plywood, and a V-tail of similar construction to the wing. The 10 hp engine is pylon-mounted aft of the pilot who sits on an exposed seat. His legs substitute for a nosewheel and two undercarriage units are carried beneath the wing. Even more unusual than the undercarriage is the control system, comprising sequentially-operated spoilers aft of the main wing spar, which cater for roll and yaw control. The TL-1A has an empty weight of 55.5 kg (122 lb) and an economic cruising speed of 64 km/h (40 mph). One hundred and eighty-six TL-1As were flying by 1980 from 458 kits of parts sold.

The Sawyer Skyjacker II, flown on 3 July 1975, has what is virtually a lifting-body configuration, with the outer panels of the short-span monoplane wings extended aft on each side of the fuselage nacelle. These are linked at their trailing-edges by a conventional tailplane with elevator, and carry ailerons outboard of the elevator. Wing endplates substitute for tailfins, and each has a yaw panel inset to serve as a rudder. The 200 hp engine is mounted in the aft of the central two-seat nacelle, driving a three-blade constant-speed pusher propeller which rotates between the outer panels of the wings and the tailplane. Maximum speed of this aircraft is 89 km/h (55 mph). With the Skyjacker II concept it

**Above:** Spratt Model 107                    **Below:** Thompson Boxmoth

**Weedhopper JC-24BL Weedhopper**

was found possible to overcome flutter and other problems associated with twin-boom designs.

Very different is the Spratt Model 107, a two-seat flying-boat with a small hull formed currently from PVC and Kevlar skin. The tail unit is of butterfly type, with no moving surfaces, and control is effected by a two-piece monoplane parasol wing. The two sections of the wing can be moved freely and collectively in incidence, and can be operated differentially for roll and directional control. Yet another pusher arrangement, it has the propeller located between the surfaces of the butterfly tail, and relies upon a long drive-shaft from the 80 hp engine.

Unique is a suitable word to describe the Thompson Boxmoth, strongly reminiscent of the pioneering attempts to build a practical aircraft based on the box kite research carried out by

Australian Lawrence Hargrave in the closing years of the 19th century. A wire-braced open frame of light alloy tubing serves to support the 55 hp engine, an underslung seat for the pilot, fixed tailwheel type undercarriage, and large rhomboidal wings fore and aft. Lateral control is by differential flexing of the main cell trailing-edges, and a rudder and all-moving elevator are mounted within the aft lifting surfaces. With a touch of the nautical, pioneered by Henri Fabre in his seaplane of 1910, the fabric panels of the wings can be furled and lashed to the centre frame when the day's flying is over, the wing spars folding also to this frame. Maximum speed of the Boxmoth is about 72 km/h (45 mph). Licences to build the Boxmoth have been issued to a number of amateur constructors.

Last of the 1975 vintage here described is the

**Mitchell Wing Model B-10**

**Mitchell Wing U-2**

**Aerocar Mini Imp**

JC-24 Weedhopper, derived from a series of hang-gliders and powered lightplanes designed by John Chotia. Its fuselage is an open triangulated structure of light alloy tubing, and with a 25 hp engine mounted at the forward end in Demoiselle style. Wingtip spoilers are used for roll control, although an alternative wing warping system is also available to homebuilders. The tail unit has conventional control surfaces. The pilot occupies an exposed seat beneath the wing. Maximum speed is 80 km/h (50 mph). By the beginning of 1980 orders for 410 kits of parts to build the Weedhopper had been received.

In 1976 the prototype Mitchell Wing Model B-10 flew for the first time as a single-seat ultralight with a tapered parasol monoplane wing. Weighing only 66 kg (145 lb) empty, and with a cruising speed of approximately 80 km/h (50 mph) on the power of a very small engine, it has become extremely popular among amateur constructors. By 1981 about 1,000 kits and sets of plans had been sold of the two versions: the B-10F foot-launched powered model and the Model B-10 powered model with a tricycle undercarriage. The Mitchell Aircraft Corporation has also plans and kits available for its U-2 single-seat ultralight, and by 1981 had received orders for 400 plans and/or kits. This aircraft was designed with the aim of developing an ultralight powered aircraft that would be superior in controllability, performance and structure to powered hang gliders. It was first flown as a prototype in 1979.

Similar in many ways to the Mitchell U-2 is the Striplin FLAC (Foot Launched Air Cycle). Flown for the first time in 1978, it is a single-seat rigid-wing powered hang glider, using a small engine with a pusher propeller. Constructed of glass-fibre, epoxy and foam, it was marketed until 1980 as a Quick Flight Kit, which required only assembly, and an Economy Kit containing all materials. The currently available version is the Super FLAC, basically similar to the original FLAC but with an enlarged pilot pod (with baggage compartment) and powered by two Soarmaster two-cylinder engines. The very latest aircraft from Striplin are the single-seat Lone Ranger and two-seat Sky Ranger.

One of the most interesting of the recent ultralights is the Hummer, designed by the late Klaus Hill, which flew for the first time in November 1977. The basic fuselage structure is an 0.13 m (5 in) diameter irrigation pipe, carrying a V-tail incorporating elevators/rudders and

**Aero Design DG-1**

the pilot's seat. Tubular struts provide mounts for the 22 hp engine with pusher propeller, and for the wire-braced monoplane wing. With a speed similar to that of the Weedhopper, it is offered to the public in the form of kits and plans. By 1980 at least twelve were flying.

There are, of course, far more sophisticated aircraft among recent designs, combining the benefits of the latest aerodynamic research with new lightweight constructional techniques. Moulton Taylor's Mini-Imp illustrates well one of the forward-looking creations, its pilot accommodated in a beautifully streamlined fuselage which has an all-metal basic structure covered by a glassfibre shell. An engine in the 60–100 hp range is mounted in the rear fuselage, and drives a pusher propeller aft of the inverted V-tail. The cantilever wings are of all-metal construction, and an electrically-retractable tricycle undercarriage is provided. With a 68 hp Limbach engine, the Mini-Imp has a cruising speed of 241 km/h (150 mph). A four-seat Imp has been under development by the parent company, Aerocar, for some time, while a version of the Mini-Imp constructed primarily of glassfibre-reinforced paper and known as the Micro-Imp flew for the first time in 1980.

Aero Design's DG-1 single-seat racing monoplane is even more revolutionary, sharing with the Mini-Imp a well-streamlined fuselage but with two 330 hp Mazda RX-3 rotary-combustion modified motor car engines mounted in 'push and pull' form. The cantilever monoplane wings, inverted rudder and ventral fin, dorsal fin and tailplane are glassfibre/foam structures, and a retractable tricycle undercarriage has been fitted. Two sets of wings have been designed for the DG-1, one set for Unlimited-class racing, enabling the aircraft to compete directly with the highly-modified P-51 Mustangs, F8F Bearcats and Hawker Sea Furies, and the other for a world speed record attempt. It has been estimated that with the record-breaking wings fitted the DG-1 should reach a maximum speed of approximately 804 km/h (500 mph), perhaps sufficient to better the current world speed record for piston-engined aircraft of 803.138 km/h (499.047 mph), set in August 1979 by a Griffon-engined P-51D Mustang.

For sheer elegance, however, the Quickie Aircraft Corporation's single-seat Quickie sporting aircraft has to be among the top of the list. Its banana-shaped fuselage is formed from foam, with glassfibre covering inside and out, sculptured to achieve the desired lines. The foam/

**Above:** The Hummer          **Below:** Striplin FLAC

**Quickie Aircraft Corporation Quickie**

glassfibre shoulder-high wings have ailerons but no flaps, while the similarly-constructed canard foreplanes have marked anhedral and incorporate full-span tapered elevator/flaps. The main undercarriage wheels are housed in swept fairings at the tips of the foreplanes, a steerable tailwheel being located below the vertical fin and rudder tail unit. Power is supplied by a modified Onan engine mounted in the nose of the fuselage, allowing a maximum speed of 225 km/h (140 mph). First flown on 15 November 1977, the Quickie proved incapable of being made to spin. It won the 'Outstanding New Design' award in 1978 at the EAA's Fly-in at Oshkosh, in which year kits became available to would-be builders. By the beginning of 1980 340 kits had been sold, with fifteen aircraft already flying.

New designs do not monopolise the scene, and typical of a creation of yesteryear is the replica of William Ramsey's Flying Bathtub of 1931, which has been built and flown by Irvin Mahugh in the USA. While duplicating the original, it uses more up-to-date constructional techniques and was good enough to be awarded the accolade 'Outstanding Replica' at the EAA's 1978 Fly-in. Powered by a 75 hp engine, it has a maximum cruising speed of 121 km/h (75 mph).

Neither should it be thought that the USA is the only source of creative homebuilts. In France aerodynamicist Michel Colomban designed a diminutive lightplane known as the Cricri, in which the two 12 hp engines are mounted close together near the nose so that the propeller slipstream deflected over the tail surfaces by the

*Above:* **Mahugh Flying Bathtub**    (*Howard Levy*)          *Below:* **Seremet W.S.12**

**Colomban Cricri**

carefully conceived shape of the cockpit canopy prevents dangerous handling problems should one engine fail. First flown on 19 July 1973, it was claimed to be the smallest twin-engined aeroplane then flying. Maximum speed is reported at 220 km/h (136 mph), although 250 km/h (155 mph) was achieved during flight tests.

More futuristic, perhaps, is the W.S.12 powered parawing, designed by W. Vincent Seremet (see the fifth chapter). This combines a Rogallo-type wing and a small turbojet engine with a controll-able exhaust nozzle. Mounted to a common frame, and strapped to the back of a pilot, flight is probably accomplished by the pilot inclining the wing about 50° upward and the exhaust nozzles about 60° downward and running forward for a few paces in order to acquire the necessary lift. Once in the air, the wing is probably realigned to a 30° angle and the exhaust nozzles to 20° for flight.

Rogallo wings are more readily associated with gliding, and both sailplanes and hang gliders include designs with uncustomary features. Hans

**Aviafiber Canard-2 FL**

**Farner HF Colibri 1 SL**

**MacCready Gossamer Albatross II** *(Martyn B. Cowley)*

Farner in Switzerland has designed and flown the Aviafiber Canard-2 FL, a single-seat ultralight sailplane constructed largely of foam material, glassfibre and laminated resin. This has a parasol monoplane wing carried on V-pylons at the rear of the fuselage, and a fixed-incidence foreplane at the nose. Twin main- and tailwheels can be jettisoned after take off. Hans Farner is the designer also of the HF Colibri 1 SL, an experimental motor glider of canard configuration which, though extremely graceful, has an unusual 'long nose'. Power is provided by two 13.6 hp engines which drive a pusher propeller aft of the wing trailing-edge.

In a lighter category come the hang gliders, a host of which are available to would-be pilots in powered and unpowered forms. These have more than brought us full circle in a review of fantastic flying machines of the amateur pilot, for their capability is far greater than that of the aircraft with which pioneers like Lilienthal, Pilcher and Chanute were flying just before the turn of the 19th century. This in no way disparages the achieve-

ments of those pioneers, for more than 80 years of advances in all of the techniques which can be applied to aircraft construction separate the two differing kinds of hang gliders.

Undoubtedly those men, and others who followed them to record the frail beginnings of powered flight, would have been fascinated by the recent achievements in man-powered flight. Space does not allow a detailed study of aircraft in this category, but one must record the achievements of Dr Paul MacCready and his team in California. His goal was to fly his Gossamer Condor, powered and piloted by Bryan Allen, around a figure-of-eight course marked by two pylons half a mile apart, to win the £50,000 Kremer Prize. This was successfully performed on 23 August 1977. Just less than two years later, on 12 June 1979, Bryan Allen was again in the 'hot seat', this time in an attempt to win the £100,000 Kremer Prize for the first man-powered flight across the English Channel. Flying Gossamer Albatross he left Folkestone at 05.51 h BST and landed on the beach at Cap Gris Nez, France, at 08.40 h, having completed

**MacCready Gossamer Penguin**     (*Don Monroe*)

the flight at speeds ranging from 17.5–24 km/h (11–15 mph) and at an average altitude of 0.5–2 m (2–6 ft) above the sea.

Another new concept in power plant for aircraft is solar power, and several people have been working to produce lightweight aircraft using this power source. Larry Mauro of California claims to be the first to have gained success with his UFM Solar Riser, a lightweight biplane based on the Easy Riser hang glider. Solar panels incorporating 300 cells give a maximum 40V 10A power output, and with associated equipment including a battery and a 3 hp electric motor, the Solar Riser recorded a solar flight in late April 1979, covering a distance of 805 m (2,640 ft).

As is usually the case with 'firsts', the Solar Riser has a challenger. In the UK Mr Freddie To designed a solar-powered aircraft as the Solar One. A short hop was claimed on 19 December 1978, and on 13 June the following year a flight of nearly three-quarters of a mile (1,200 m) was made, reaching a maximum speed of about 65 km/h (40 mph). Solar One uses batteries to power the four 1 hp electric motors that drive a single tractor-mounted propeller above the nose, and which store energy supplied by 750 solar cells attached to the upper surface of the root section of the wings.

Paul MacCready has also been working along similar lines, and following considerable test and research his Gossamer Penguin recorded a solar flight of about 3 km (2 miles) on 7 August 1980. The Solar Challenger, with some 16,000 photovoltaic cells, managed the first solar-powered flight across the English Channel on 7 July 1981.

There are the inevitable 'jokers' who ask what will happen if the sun becomes obscured by cloud in mid-Channel. They have been with us throughout aviation history, but have never succeeded in stopping the creation of many ideas which have occasionally failed to the echo of their laughter. But the thinkers of strange ideas, and the builders of even stranger shapes, have already contributed a great deal to aerospace progress. May they long continue to do so!

# 7. Superlatives

On 26 April 1939 24-year-old test pilot Flugkapitän Fritz Wendel gained the world absolute speed record, achieving the officially recognised speed of 755.138 km/h (469.22 mph) at Augsburg in Germany. His aircraft was the Messerschmitt Me 209 V1, a 2,300 hp Daimler-Benz DB 601ARJ-engined 'one-off', contrary to spurious German propaganda that attempted to convince onlookers that it was a version of the latest German single-seat fighter and as such designated Bf 109R. This record was the last to be set before the outbreak of World War II, and bettered the previous record set one week earlier by the Heinkel He 100.

The advances achieved during the war enabled a British Gloster Meteor F4 jet fighter to set the first post-war record at more than 970 km/h (600 mph), but greater goals lay ahead. Back in 1943 design work had begun on the Miles M-52, a projected jet-powered research aircraft intended to fly at speeds of up to 1,609 km/h (1,000 mph) at an altitude of 10,975 m (36,000 ft). By early 1946 approximately 90% of the design work had been completed and construction of a full-size aircraft was underway. However, although intended to fly that year, the M-52 project was cancelled. It was believed, mistakenly, that the M-52 should have been fitted with swept wings, and doubts in design and the possibility of supersonic flight, combined with economic restrictions, ended Britain's bid for the first supersonic aircraft. Interestingly, trials with Vickers-built models of the M-52 proved subsequently that the aircraft could have achieved its purpose.

Withdrawal of the M-52 left the USA with the best chance of gaining this important 'first'. Although in the 1950s McDonnell attempted to produce a supersonic propeller design, tested on its XF-88B with turbojets in the rear fuselage for normal power and a nose-mounted Allison XT38 turboprop for research, Bell, in the 1940s, selected a rear-mounted reaction motor for its X-1 aeroplane.

**McDonnell XF-88B**

**Bell X-1**  (*Bell Helicopter Textron*)

**Charles 'Chuck' Yeager in the cockpit of the Bell X-1**

**Bell X-2**

Unlike the British aircraft, the X-1 used a 2,720 kg (6,000 lb) thrust bi-propellant rocket motor (Reaction Motors E6000-C4) and was intended for air-launching from a Boeing B-29 Superfortress bomber 'motherplane'. Altogether three X-1s were built, the first unpowered air-launch taking place on 19 January 1946. Powered flights began that December.

As if to rub salt in British wounds, the X-1 had a similar straight wing layout as planned for the M-52; on 14 October 1947 Captain Charles Yeager piloted the aircraft to 1,078 km/h (670 mph) at 12,800 m (42,000 ft) altitude. Representing a speed of Mach 1.015, the sound barrier had been broken.

One X-1, modified to incorporate turbo-driven fuel pumps, a new cockpit canopy, longer fuselage and increased fuel capacity, as the X-1A, went on to achieve a staggering Mach 2.435 on 12 December 1953, and in June of the following year attained an altitude of more than 27,430 m (90,000 ft). During the course of the X-1 programme, covering modifications up to X-1E form, 156 flights were made, punctuated by the destruction of the X-1D on its first flight, when it was jettisoned from the B-50 'motherplane' following an explosion. Not only had the USA proved that flying at the speed of sound was possible but had triumphed over Mach 2 with a straight-winged aeroplane.

To explore further the problems associated with transonic and supersonic flight, Bell followed the X-1 with the swept-wing X-2. The wings and tail were of stainless steel and power was provided by a throttlable Curtiss-Wright XLR25-CW-1 liquid-propellant rocket motor. Intended to be air-launched from a Boeing B-50 'motherplane', it was provided with a nosewheel and flat skid undercarriage. Two X-2s were constructed, the first going the way of the X-1D when, in May 1954, it was jettisoned from the B-50 after being damaged by an explosion in the bomber. The second X-2 was more successful and made a powered flight on 18 November 1955. On 7 September 1956, following other flights, Captain Iven Kincheloe, USAF, flew the aircraft to an altitude of 36,637 m (126,200 ft). Nearly three weeks later, on 27 September, Captain Milburn Apt, USAF, flew the X-2 at

**Bell X-2 beneath the B-50 'motherplane'**

the hitherto-unprecedented speed of 3,370 km/h (2,094 mph), representing Mach 3.2. Unfortunately, the triumphant flight ended in tragedy when the X-2 crashed, killing the pilot.

Although the Bell X-1 and X-2 flew faster than any other aircraft during their respective test programmes, their speeds were not officially ratified as records as they did not take-off from the earth's surface under their own power. As mentioned at the beginning of this chapter, the British Gloster Meteor F4 held the absolute world speed record for the first two years of peace, progressively increasing it during this period. Then, on 19 June 1947, America gained the record for the first time since the 1920s, achieving 1,003.6 km/h (623.61 mph) with its Lockheed P-80R Shooting Star fighter. Sandwiched between this record and those set from 1948 to 1953 by the North American F-86 Sabre fighter were two set by the Douglas

D-558-1 Skystreak. First flown on 28 May 1947, the Skystreak was a fairly conventional research aircraft, powered by an Allison J35 turbojet engine and designed to obtain in free flight air-load measurements not obtainable in wind-tunnels of the time. For this an automatic pressure-recording system was fitted, with 400 measurement points on the fuselage, wings and tail. Strain gauges were fitted to selected points on the tail and wings. Three Skystreaks were built to US Navy Bureaù of Aeronautics and NACA order, the first setting a world speed record at Muroc Dry Lake of 1,030.95 km/h (640.60 mph) on 20 August 1947. Five days later it raised it to 1,047.33 km/h (650.78 mph).

The original Skystreak contract was modified shortly after work had begun to include investigation of sweptback wings at very high speed. As the turbojet-powered Skystreak was incapable of the

**Douglas D-558-1 Skystreak**    (*McDonnell Douglas*)

**Douglas D-558-2 Skyrocket**    (*McDonnell Douglas*)

*Above:* **Nord Gerfaut IA**          *Below:* **Fairey Delta 2**

necessary performance, Douglas produced three D-558-2 Skyrockets, each with a 1,360 kg (3,000 lb) thrust Westinghouse J34-WE-22 turbojet engine and a 2,720 kg (6,000 lb) thrust Reaction Motors XLR-8 bi-propellant rocket motor. The first flew on 4 February 1948. In August 1951 a Skyrocket, with its turbojet engine removed and fuel increased, achieved 1,992 km/h (1,238 mph), having been air-launched. Following other dramatic flights by the Skyrockets, on 20 November 1953 one accelerated to Mach 2.005 after being air-launched at 9,755 m (32,000 ft), recording the first flight of a manned aircraft at twice the speed of sound. As with the Bell aircraft, this could not be ratified officially as an absolute world speed record. Nevertheless, the USA had, by 1956, set 'firsts' for Mach 1, Mach 2 and Mach 3, and flights with the X-15 were still to come!

At about the same time France was experimenting with several interesting aircraft, some of which are mentioned in the final chapter. On 15 January 1954 the first flight took place of the Nord Gerfaut IA, a research aircraft designed to collect data for the future development of a high-speed fighter. It was the first high-powered jet (4,400 kg; 9,700 lb thrust SNECMA Atar 101G) with delta-wings to fly

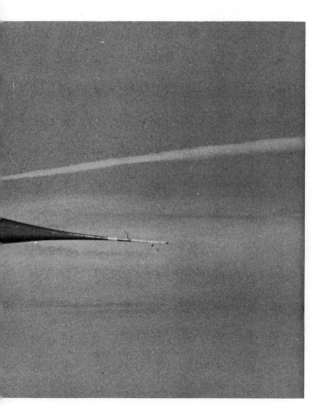

in France. On 3 August that year it exceeded Mach 1 in level flight, to become the first aircraft in Europe to fly faster than sound without the use of an afterburner or rocket power. The Gerfaut IA was followed by the IB, with larger wings and other improvements, and the Gerfaut II. The Gerfaut II established several time-to-height records from a standing start on 16 February 1957, and was capable of Mach 1.3 at 12,000 m (39,375 ft) altitude.

Meanwhile, in Britain the Miles M-52 project had long been forgotten and by 1954 national pride centred upon two aircraft. The first was the Hawker Hunter jet fighter, which had broken the North American F-86 Sabre's hold on the world speed record during the previous year and was now entering RAF squadrons, and the second was the Fairey Delta 2.

Connected only to the earlier Fairey F.D.1 by its parent company, the Delta 2 was designed primarily to investigate the characteristics of flight and control at transonic and supersonic speeds. Powered by a 5,443 kg (12,000 lb) thrust Rolls-Royce Avon RA.5 in the first aircraft and by a 5,896 kg (13,000 lb) thrust Avon RA.28 in the second, it was an extremely graceful aircraft with delta wings using Fairey symmetrical wing section, a long pointed fuselage, and a special nose section which could pivot downward to improve the pilot's view during take-off and landing.

The first aircraft took off for the first time on 6 October 1954 but was damaged in a landing accident on 17 November. Repaired, it was to give Britain its long awaited 'first' when, on 10 March 1956, it was flown by Peter Twiss at an average speed over two runs of 1,821.39 km/h (1,131.76 mph), setting not only a world speed record but the first of over 1,000 mph. This easily bettered the 1,323.03 km/h (822.09 mph) of the North American F-100C Super Sabre. During the early 1960s it was redesigned and almost completely rebuilt as the BAC 221 for use by the Royal Aircraft Establishment. It was finally retired after a last flight on 9 June 1973, having been involved in several research programmes and contributing to the development of the Concorde supersonic airliner.

In the year that the first Skystreak flew Douglas received another contract for a research aircraft, designated X-3. Designed to research into the efficiency of turbojet engines and very short-span

**BAC 221**   (*Air Portraits*)

**Douglas X-3**   (*McDonnell Douglas*)

**North American X-15**

**Bristol T.188**

double-wedge wings and tailplanes, and to provide data on thermodynamic heating at speeds of up to Mach 3 and at high altitudes, it was of very interesting configuration. The long slim fuselage had a pointed nose and a thin tailboom supporting the tail surfaces. An intake for the two 1,905 kg (4,200 lb) thrust Westinghouse J34-WE-17 turbojet engines was mounted each side of the fuselage aft of the pilot's cabin. More than 850 'pin-hole' orifices recorded pressures over the airframe, while temperatures, stresses and air loads were also measured.

Construction of the X-3 presented engineers with problems to solve of unprecedented complexity, not only in matters of aerodynamics but in the use of new materials including titanium. Actual construction began in 1949 and the first flight was achieved on 20 October 1952. The research programme was ended on 23 May 1956, following nearly three years with NACA. Interestingly, the long thin fuselage and short-span wing layout was adopted soon after the X-3's first flight by Lockheed for its revolutionary F-104 Starfighter jet fighter.

Ten years after the first flight of the X-3, Britain tested its own research aircraft designed to achieve Mach 3. First flown on 14 April 1962, the Bristol T.188 had been built to Ministry of Aviation contract. It was of stainless steel construction, with two 6,350 kg (14,000 lb) thrust (with reheat) Bristol Siddeley Gyron Junior DGJ.10R turbojet engines mounted in long nacelles in the wings. Two flying aircraft (plus one airframe for structural testing) were completed, intended initially to investigate prolonged flight at speeds of up to Mach 3, and also to test armament and other propulsion systems, although defence applications were subsequently modified in accordance with changed government policy. Certainly the T.188's development and aerodynamic testing was seen mainly as a contribution to the future design of the supersonic transport aircraft. Results obtained from the T.188 programme were not released, although it is known that the tests were ended early due to the aircraft's high rate of fuel consumption. Maximum level speed achieved was more than 1,931 km/h (1,200 mph).

The two final superlatives to be mentioned in this chapter originated from North American Aviation – the first a rocket-powered research aircraft and the second a strategic bomber. In

**North American X-15A-2**

1955 North American announced that it had received a USAF/USN/NACA contract to build three manned research aircraft with a design speed of at least Mach 7 and capable of an altitude of 80,500 m (264,000 ft). It is worth noting at this point that in 1955 the world speed record (official) was held by the F-100C (see earlier paragraph) and the altitude record stood at 20,083 m (65,889 ft). The hypersonic research aircraft were intended to furnish data relating to heating, stability, control and the problems of re-entry into the atmosphere. Scepticism from onlookers was still rife when the first X-15A flew attached to the underwing of its Boeing B-52 Stratofortress 'motherplane' on 10 March 1959. On 8 June the first unpowered free flight was achieved, followed on 17 September by a powered flight by the second aircraft. Although the intended power plant for the aircraft was the

Thiokol (Reaction Motors) XLR99 single-chamber throttlable liquid-propellant rocket motor, this was not ready for the initial tests and so two 3,630 kg (8,000 lb) thrust LR11-RM-5 rocket motors were substituted. From May 1960 the X-15As achieved successively higher speeds: Mach 3.19 on 12 May 1960, Mach 4.43 on 7 March 1961, Mach 5.27 on 23 June 1961 and Mach 6.04 on 9 November 1961. Following an accident to No 2, this aircraft was rebuilt in a new form, with additional propellants carried in large external tanks under each side of the fuselage. As the X-15A-2, powered by a 25,855 kg (57,000 lb) thrust XLR99-RM-2 motor, it achieved Mach 5.92 on 27 June 1962, and finally the yet unbeaten Mach 6.72 on 3 October 1967, the latter representing a speed of 7,297 km/h (4,534 mph). On 17 July 1962 the X-15A-3 achieved an altitude of 95,935.99 m (314,750 ft), while on 22 August

**North American XB-70A Valkyrie**

the following year 107,960 m (354,200 ft) was reached.

Built largely of stainless steel and titanium, the X-15 airframe was covered in an armoured skin of Inconel X nickel alloy steel, to withstand temperatures of +1,200°F to −300°F. Higher temperatures were reached by the X-15A-2 following coating of the airframe with Emerson Electric T-500 ablative material. Control at high altitudes was achieved by means of twelve jet nozzles of the HTP rocket type, eight in the nose and two in each wingtip. In total, 199 X-15 flights were made, the programme ending in November 1968, one year after X-15A-3 had been lost in a crash in California.

The second North American aircraft was entirely different, representing one of the most advanced strategic bombers ever built, certainly the fastest, and arguably the most incredible. Designated XB-70 for the USAF and named Valkyrie, its overall length was 59.74 m (196 ft). Powered by six 14,060 kg (31,000 lb) thrust (with afterburning) General Electric YJ93-GE-3 turbojet engines, it was designed to fly the entire distance to and from its target at Mach 3, having a range of 12,230 km (7,600 miles). Special design features included delta wings of very thin section, wingtips that could fold down hydraulically

to an angle of 25° for low-altitude supersonic flight and to 65° for high-altitude Mach 3 cruising flight (to improve stability and manoeuvrability), and twelve elevons in the trailing-edges of the wings.

Intended as a Boeing B-52 replacement, the XB-70 was cancelled as a bomber project in 1963, allowing the available money for new equipment to be spent on strategic missiles. Instead just two were built as XB-70A aerodynamic test aircraft, the first flying on 21 September 1964. Mach 1 was exceeded on the third flight and Mach 3 achieved on 14 October 1965. On 8 June 1966 the second aircraft was lost when it was involved in a collision with its Lockheed F-104 Starfighter chase aircraft. The original XB-70A went on to complete 71 flights by early 1968, and in the following year the programme was terminated.

It is an unfortunate fact that it appears likely we shall never see again new aircraft of X-15 or Valkyrie calibre built purely for research, such is the high cost of development, materials and fuel. On the positive side we must be thankful that most of the aircraft mentioned in this chapter have been preserved in museums for future generations to view and admire.

# 8. Shapes

Each of the previous chapters has centred on a theme. In this final chapter it is intended to present aircraft of all shapes, sizes and purposes, linked only by one common fact – they all have flown!

During World War II the Douglas Aircraft Company busied itself producing military aircraft for the Allies. At its peak of production it employed 150,000 persons, 50% women, and, based on total structural weight, was responsible for one-sixth of all US national military aircraft production during 1943–44. Over the period 1944–45 it was engaged mainly in constructing two- and four-engined transports and twin-engined bombers for the USAAF and US Navy. During 1944 manufacture of the Havoc and Dauntless ended (July and September respectively), but output of the C-54 Skymaster (DC-4), C-47 Skytrain (DC-3) and A-26 Invader was stepped up to meet the increasing demands of the fighting forces. Douglas also co-operated in the construction of Boeing B-17 Flying Fortress bombers.

Towards the end of the war Douglas began thinking again of commercial transports, projecting the use of the DC-4, DC-6, DC-7 and DC-8. The DC-8, as mentioned in the 1945–46 *Jane's*

**Douglas XB-42 Mixmaster**

**Douglas XB-42A Mixmaster**

*All the World's Aircraft*, was a projected twin-engined transport monoplane incorporating the novel engine installation originally designed for the XA-42 attack aircraft, using two Allison piston engines in the fuselage driving contra-rotating propellers aft of the tail unit, the aircraft itself accommodating 38 passengers.

In retrospect we know that the DC-8 'pusher' transport was never built, and seldom (if ever) is it mentioned in histories, but the XA-42 was of great interest. Two flying prototypes and a ground test model were ordered by the US Air Technical Service Command on 25 June 1943, the intention being to produce an aircraft capable of carrying various combinations of guns – ranging from eight 0.50 in to one 75 mm cannon and two 0.50 in guns – and bombs for attack

duties. Before the first flew on 6 May 1944, the aircraft had been redesignated XB-42 Mixmaster as a bomber with a designed warload of 907 kg (2,000 lb) and a range of 6,440 km (4,000 miles). The second flying prototype took off for the first time on 1 August 1944. Apart from the unusual engine/propeller layout the XB-42 had cruciform tail surfaces with twin fins and rudders, the first aircraft also having two blister canopies for the pilots side-by-side near the fuselage nose. On 8 December the same year the first aircraft flew from Long Beach, California, to Washington, DC, covering the 3,685 kms (2,290 miles) at an average speed of 695 km/h (432 mph).

With the end of World War II in sight, hopes to put the XB-42 into production were ended. On 15 December 1945 one of the two aircraft crashed, through no fault of either the airframe or power plant installation. But now most major post-war air forces were considering (or had begun) converting from piston-engined fighters and bombers to jet-powered types. The XB-42 still offered great potential as a medium bomber, especially with its proved range of about 8,047 km (5,000 miles), but to attract orders it needed turbojet power. As an interim, the remaining XB-42 was given two 725 kg (1,600 lb) thrust Westinghouse 19XB-2A turbojets to supplement the 1,725 hp Allison V-1710s. The resulting aircraft was redesignated XB-42A, and flew for the first time on 27 May 1947.

From the XB-42A was developed the XB-43, the two examples built becoming the USAF's first jet bombers (although experimental). The XB-43 had a shorter fuselage and greater span than the XB-42/XB-42A, a conventional tail unit and two 1,814 kg (4,000 lb) thrust General Electric TG-180 turbojets in the rear fuselage. This version also failed to attract orders, but nevertheless fully deserves its place in aviation history.

One of the most colourful characters in pre-World War II aviation was Howard Hughes, then a young multi-millionaire businessman, sportsman and film producer. He was the holder of aeroplane speed and distance records, and his aircraft company was among the first to experi-ment with plastic materials for aircraft construction. In 1942 Howard Hughes joined with Henry J. Kaiser to build three experimental cargo-carrying flying-boats for the US government. Henry Kaiser, a prominent shipbuilder, is often remembered in aviation circles for offering to build 5,000 Martin Mars four-engined flying-boats in his shipyards, suggesting that full production could be underway within ten months. This proposal was proved unmanageable, but the three eight-engined flying-boats ordered by the government were to prove equally challenging, as they were to be of original design. Moreover, the first was to be completed in 15 months for static trials, the second and third in 20 and 25 months for flight trials. Construction was to be entirely of wood; the engines, propellers and instruments were to have been supplied by the War and Navy Departments.

In the event delays and difficulties pushed back the work schedule. Gradually the Aircraft and War Production Boards became sceptical about the project, partly due to preliminary tests which revealed that the completed flying-boat was likely to be very much overweight. In early 1944 the project was cancelled, one reason given being that concern over shortages of strategic materials had been unfounded. As consolation it was suggested that one of the wooden

**Hughes H-4 Hercules**

**Douglas XB-43**    *(US Air Force)*

hulls could be used as a mock-up to determine the worth of building a similar flying-boat in metal.

Howard Hughes was not a man to be diverted from his chosen path and continued to build one aircraft at his own expense. Reportedly spending more than $25 million on completion of his Hughes H-4 Hercules, the flying-boat became the biggest aeroplane ever built, weighing in at about 181,436 kg (400,000 lb) and with a wing span of 97.536 m (320 ft). Using special trailering equipment, parts of the Hercules were transported by road in mid-1946 from Culver City to Long Beach, California, in preparation for final assembly. On 2 November the following year the Hercules made its one and only flight at the hands of Howard Hughes, covering about one mile (1.6 km) at very low altitude over Los Angeles harbour, reputedly partly to win Hughes a small wager. Powered by eight 3,000 hp Pratt & Whitney R-4360 Wasp Major engines, the aircraft might have carried up to 700 passengers instead of freight. After the flight, it was taken back to its hangar, where it remained until recently.

Within a year of the Hercules flight another important US aircraft took to the air. This was the Convair Model 7002, the world's first true delta-winged aircraft. Designed as a flying mock-up for the projected XF-92 mixed power fighter, it had small delta wings with 60° sweepback on the leading-edges and 6½% thickness/chord ratio. Power was provided initially by a 2,086 kg (4,600 lb) thrust Allison J33-A-23 turbojet engine. Collaborating in design and development was Dr Alexander Lippisch, who had undertaken research along similar lines in Germany before and during World War II.

Following cancellation of the XF-92 fighter, the Model 7002 was given the designation XF-92A. It flew for the first time on 18 September 1948. In 1951 the original engine was changed for a 3,720 kg (8,200 lb) thrust J33-A-29 with afterburner, allowing very high subsonic speeds (Mach 0.95) to be attained. In 1952 it was handed over to NACA for continued research, having completed its evaluation programme with the USAF.

From the XF-92A was developed the Convair

**Convair XF-92A**  *(General Dynamics)*

**Avro 707B**

F-102 Delta Dagger fighter, which first flew on 24 October 1953 as basically a 1.22:1 scale-up of the research aircraft. Many other aircraft benefited from the XF-92A programme in one way or another.

Britain was only a 'short head' behind the US in delta research, having flown its Avro Type 707 low- and high-speed delta-wing research aircraft for the first time on 4 September 1949. Indeed, the world's first delta-winged jet bomber was the British Avro Vulcan, the five Type 707s having been instrumental in its development.

During the 1940s and 1950s France was a veritable 'hotbed' of original research. Those pro-

duced by, or best remembered as products of, Sud-Est Aviation and Sud-Ouest Aviation are of particular interest. The genealogy of the companies is interesting, the former known until September 1956 as Société Nationale de Constructions Aéronautiques du Sud-Est (SNCASE) and the latter as Société Nationale de Constructions Aéronautiques de Sud-Ouest (SNCASO), following nationalisation of the French aircraft industry in 1937. In March 1957 Sud-Est and Sud-Ouest merged to form Sud-Aviation, later to become part of the present Aérospatiale concern.

The Sud-Ouest SO 6000 Triton, first flown on 11 November 1946, was a side-by-side two-seat

**Above:** Sud-Ouest SO 6000 Triton          **Below:** Sud-Ouest SO 6025 Espadon

experimental trainer. Powered initially by a German Junkers Jumo 004 B2 turbojet engine, it was the first jet-propelled aircraft to fly in France, having been developed from 1943 in secrecy while the country was still under German occupation. Construction of a prototype had begun in 1945. Four subsequent prototypes were all powered by 2,200 kg (4,850 lb) thrust Hispano-Suiza-built Rolls-Royce Nene 101 turbojets, the first taking to the air on 19 March 1948.

Other memorable Sud-Ouest designs were the Espadon, SO M.2 and SO 9000 Trident. The Espadon originated as an experimental interceptor, built to the specifications of the first French post-war official military aircraft programme. With sweptback wings and powered by a Hispano-Suiza-built Rolls-Royce Nene turbojet engine, the first prototype flew initially on 12 November 1948. It was followed by two other interceptor/fighter prototypes built under the SO 6020 designation.

The SO 6021 was also a combat type, developed as a lighter version of the second prototype, with a smaller pressurised and air conditioned cockpit, ejector seat, increased wing area and armed with six 20 mm or four 30 mm cannon. First flown in September 1950, it was reported subsequently to have exceeded Mach 0.95 in a dive. Meanwhile the programme had been extended to include research. The third prototype was modified to include some SO 6021 features, plus provision for cameras in the nose and an SEPR 251 bi-propellant rocket motor under the fuselage. In this form it flew on 28 December 1949. The last version of the Espadon was the SO 6026 of 1951, in fact the modified second prototype with a rocket motor in the rear fuselage under the jet tailpipe. In the following year the first prototype was fitted with wingtip-mounted Turboméca Marboré turbojet engines for research, no doubt to evaluate this engine layout before the first flight of the SO 9000 Trident.

Design of the Trident began in 1948 but the contract for development of a prototype was not received until 1951. First flight was, therefore, delayed until 2 March 1953. Initially the aircraft was powered by two 400 kg (880 lb) thrust Turboméca Marboré II turbojet engines mounted at the tips of the short-span, constant-chord, straight wings. The aircraft's tail surfaces were

**Sud-Ouest SO 9050 Trident II**

made up of three one-piece all-moving planes: the vertical plane acted as a rudder, and the tailplane had marked anhedral and provided both roll and pitch control. Interestingly, the complete nose of the Trident could be jettisoned in an emergency.

As flight testing progressed a 4,500 kg (9,920 lb) thrust SEPR 481 rocket motor was installed in the rear fuselage, the aircraft making a flight with rocket power on 4 September 1954. Soon after the Marboré engines were replaced by wingtip-mounted 745 kg (1,640 lb) thrust Dassault M.D.30 Viper ASV.5 turbojets, flying resuming on 18 March the following year. Within a short time the Trident had easily exceeded the speed of sound in a dive on turbojet power alone, and on 3 April 1955 it exceeded Mach 1 in a climb while using a fraction of the available power from its rocket motor. Test flights were conducted at speeds of up to 1,700 km/h (1,056 mph). A second Trident had also been built, but this had crashed on its first flight in September 1953.

From the SO 9000 was developed the SO 9050 Trident II prototype lightweight mixed-power interceptor, a contract for two examples having been signed in 1954. The first flew initially on 19 July 1955 on the power of its turbojet engines alone, using rocket power for the first time on 21

**Sud-Est Grognard**

December that year. However, one Trident II was destroyed on 21 May 1957 when the rocket fuels mixed accidentally in the air.

Shortly before the accident, on 3 May, the first of six pre-production Trident IIs flew for the first time. Able to be powered by either Dassault M.D.30 Viper ASV.5 or 1,100 kg (2,425 lb) thrust Turboméca Gabizo turbojets, plus the 3,000 kg (6,610 lb) thrust SEPR 631 rocket motor, the pre-production aircraft had a maximum speed of Mach 1.95. On 2 May 1956 a Gabizo-powered Trident II set an aeroplane altitude record of 24,300 m (79,724 ft), but this proved to be the last flight of a Trident II, the programme having been cancelled for economic reasons.

Unlike the Trident and Espadon, designed as interceptors, the SO M.2 was built as a half-scale model of the planned SO 4000 bomber. It followed the SO M.1 glider and first flew on 13 April 1949. In May the following year it became the first French aircraft to exceed 1,000 km/h in level flight, beating the SO 6021 Espadon's attempt at the speed by several months. Powered by one 1,587 kg (3,500 lb) thrust Rolls-Royce Derwent 5 turbojet engine, its most unusual feature was its undercarriage, made up of a nosewheel, three wheels in tandem beneath the fuselage and small wheels near the wingtips. The M.2 went into a second test phase in September 1951, recent modifications including provision for fitting solid-propellant rockets for thrust augmentation. However, the SO 4000 bomber programme was abandoned.

Sud-Est's contribution to the experimental military aircraft scene in France around 1950 was the Grognard, designed for evaluation in a ground attack role. Special features included a uniquely humped upper fuselage containing two 2,200 kg (4,850 lb) thrust Hispano-Suiza-built Rolls-Royce Nene 101 turbojet engines, swept-back wings and a heavily-glazed cockpit for the pilot in the extreme nose. Two examples were built, as the single-seat SE 2410, which first flew on 30 April 1950, and the two-seat SE 2415 Grognard II, flying on 14 February 1951. The later version had also a longer forward fuselage,

**Nord 1500 Griffon II**    *(R. A. Cole)*

**Fouga C.M.88-R Gemeaux**

redesigned cockpit enclosure and less heavily swept wing leading-edges. Both were used primarily as armament testbeds, carrying out trials with many weapons, including air-to-air missiles. A fully equipped all-weather fighter version of the Grognard was planned as the SE 2421, but this was abandoned before a prototype had been built.

Several other aircraft of French extraction are worthy of mention. The Fouga C.M.88-R Gemeaux was a very interesting experimental aircraft, built by joining the fuselages and outer wings of two Cyclope aircraft by a centre-wing and aft connecting member to produce a flying testbed for Turboméca turbojet engines. The Nord 1500 Griffon was another, produced to flight test a new airframe design embodying a combination turbojet-ramjet propulsion unit. The Griffon I made its first flight on 20 September 1955 on the power of the SNECMA Atar 101F turbojet engine with afterburner originally fitted. Eventually the airframe was modified to take a 3,500 kg (7,716 lb) thrust SNECMA Atar 101E3 turbojet mounted inside a 1.37 m (4 ft 6 in) diameter integral ramjet of Nord design, just forward of the ramjet burners. Although basically

the same aircraft, the re-engined version was named Griffon II and flew initially on 23 January 1957. On 17 May that year it exceeded Mach 1 with its ramjet ignited, but on limited power, and during the course of more than 200 flights achieved a maximum speed of Mach 2.19 or 2,316 km/h (1,448 mph). Higher speeds were prevented only by the thermal limitations of the airframe.

Earlier experiments with athodyd or ramjet power plants in France had been successfully conducted by René Leduc. He had begun experimenting in the early 1930s and in 1935 developed a small unit capable of producing 4 kg (8.82 lb) thrust at 300 m/sec (984 ft/sec), the speed rating indicating that a ramjet engine can only operate when sufficient air velocity is introduced into the tube. After the war he produced the two-seat Leduc 0.10 aircraft, first released as a glider from the back of a specially-adapted SE 161 Languedoc transport aircraft (in October 1947) and then released for a powered flight on 21 April 1949. The 0.10 left the carrier transport at a speed of 320 km/h (200 mph), accelerating during its 12 minute flight to 680 km/h (422 mph). On a later flight a speed of 805 km/h (500 mph) was achieved at 11,000 m (36,100 ft) altitude while using only half the power available from the 2,000 kg (4,410 lb) thrust Leduc engine.

A second 0.10 was built, like the first having a tubular double-skinned fuselage. The inner fuselage shell contained the pilot's cockpit, while the outer shell formed the annular duct for the ramjet. Injector pumps and a generator were positioned aft of the cockpit, powered by an auxiliary gas turbine engine, behind which were five cylindrical ducts of increasing size. The leading-edge of each duct was ringed with fuel injectors, with a total of 500 burners. In operation, as air entered the annular opening of the fuselage, it was channelled to the centre where it entered the cylindrical ducts. Gases produced by ignition of the resultant mixture were ejected from the rear of the fuselage as a high-velocity jet, the engine igniting from the auxiliary gas turbine.

From the 0.10 was developed the 0.16, differing mainly in having additional wingtip-mounted Turboméca turbojet engines. First flown on 8 February 1951, this aircraft was not entirely successful and did most of its flying with the turbojets removed. By now the French Air Ministry was

**Leduc 0.10 carried by a specially-adapted Languedoc airliner**

**Leduc 0.21**

becoming extremely interested in the Leduc experiments, culminating in an order for two 0.21s. Powered by a 6,500 kg (14,330 lb) thrust ramjet (rated at 1,000 km/h; 621 mph), each single-seat 0.21 was about one-third larger than the 0.10 but still had to be air-launched. The first flight of an 0.21 was achieved on 16 May 1953 and subsequent trials were very successful. The Ministry was now sure that the ramjet power plant and other components tested on the 0.21s were sufficiently developed to risk construction of two further aircraft, but this time as 0.22 military interceptor prototypes with Mach 2 performance. The first 0.22 took to the air initially on 26 December 1956, its auxiliary Turboméca Atar D.3 turbojet engine allowing take-off from the ground. However, in the following year the 0.22 programme was cancelled as part of the cutbacks in military spending.

In Britain in 1943 a committee was set up under Lord Brabazon of Tara (known as the Brabazon Committee) to advise on the types of civil aircraft most suited for production immediately after World War II. One aircraft resulting from the Committee's work was the Bristol Type 167, best remembered as the Brabazon. It was intended as a trans-ocean airliner with a still-air range of 8,050 km (5,000 miles) and an economical cruising speed of 402 km/h (250 mph). To be powered by eight Bristol engines totally enclosed in the huge 70.1 m (230 ft) span wings, driving four contra-rotating propellers, it was to accommodate a maximum of 244 passengers by day and 80 by night, plus freight, mail and baggage. The flight deck, passenger cabins and cargo holds were to be air-conditioned and pressurised.

Two prototypes and up to ten production Brabazons were sanctioned for construction in stages, provided the design work and later construction did not detract from military aircraft production necessary to win the war. The obvious goal with the Brabazon was to operate the direct London to New York service without having to refuel en route in the west-bound direction. The first prototype was known as the Brabazon Mk 1 and was powered by eight 2,500 hp Bristol Centaurus 20 radial engines. It began flight trials on 4 September 1949. The plan was to use this first aircraft for experimental flight research into the problems associated with very large aircraft, leaving the Bristol Proteus turboprop-engined Mk 2 to be furnished as a 100-passenger airliner. In the event, although the Brabazon Mk 1 flew well and BEA wanted to operate it between London and Nice, France, fatigue cracks in the propeller mounting and other problems brought the

**Bristol Brabazon**

whole Brabazon project to an end. The Mk 2 was therefore never built, but might have achieved a cruising speed of 531 km/h (330 mph).

Interestingly, a similar fate attended the British Saunders-Roe Princess, a huge flying-boat powered by ten 3,780 shp Bristol Proteus 600 Series turboprop engines and accommodating between 105 and 220 passengers. Like the Brabazon it was seen as ideal for the likely post-war boom in air travel across the Atlantic to New York, and three prototypes were ordered against great interest by BOAC. The first Princess took to the air in August 1952 and began flight trials, which proved very successful. The remaining prototypes were not completed immediately as they were awaiting Bristol Proteus 705 engines. By the time these engines became available all advan-

tages of flying-boats for long-range transport had been lost to new landplanes and the Princess was cancelled.

A British aircraft intended from the beginning for aerodynamic research only was the Handley Page H.P.115, which first flew on 17 August 1961. Built to a Ministry of Aviation contract, it had a wing of slender, low aspect ratio delta planform. The 862 kg (1,900 lb) thrust Bristol Siddeley Viper 9 turbojet engine was mounted above the rear of the fuselage, on top of which were the fin and rudder. For its flight programme the aircraft had a wing with a leading-edge sweep of 74° 42′ and without any form of conical camber or ogival planform; but the leading-edge was detachable to permit flight testing of different shapes if required. A fairing on the tailfin housed a camera

**Above: Saunders-Roe Princess**

**Below: Handley Page H.P.115**

1

**Fairchild Pack-Plane** (*US Air Force*)

to photograph wool tufts on the wing during flight. It provided a great deal of information useful to the Anglo-French Concorde supersonic airliner project, allowing practical flying experience with a wing of this type.

Transport aircraft with detachable lower fuselages (normally known as pods or packs) have interested military planners for several decades. Seeing the military advantages of airlifting a self-contained pack into a forward area carrying cargo, troops, field hospital or command/communications equipment, releasing it on the ground or air-dropping it during a low altitude flyover, and in either case allowing the aircraft to return to base for another mission, several attempts have been made to produce a practical design. Today the US forces fly the Sikorsky CH-54 Tarhe (S-64 Skycrane) helicopter for such missions, while the Soviet Kamov Ka-26 has a similar capability, but in the 1940s helicopter technology could not provide the goods.

In the late 1940s the USAF placed a contract with Fairchild for an experimental detachable-fuselage transport aircraft, subsequently known as the XC-120 Pack-Plane. Fairchild was in the happy position of being able to use wings, 3,250 hp Pratt & Whitney R-4360 radial engines, tailbooms and a tail unit similar to those of its C-119 Packet transport. These were married to a new shallow fuselage nacelle with a flat bottom, which housed the crew of five in the forward section. Under the nacelle could be attached the detachable fuselage or pack, which was raised and lowered by four electrically-operated hoists built into the carrier. Four dual-wheel handling gear units, fitted to the pack before lowering to the ground, allowed a vehicle to tow the pack away. The space between the pack and the carrier aircraft was sealed by an inflatable rubber tube for flight.

First flown on 11 August 1950, the Pack-Plane proved successful during flight trials. The pack measured 11.25 m (36 ft 11 in) long, 2.79 m (9 ft 2 in) wide and 2.44 m (8 ft) high, and had a volume of 82.12m³ (2,900 cu ft). But, despite its promise, the Pack-Plane never went into production.

An aircraft with a detachable under fuselage of very different type was the Aerocar Model I, designed as a convertible aeroplane and road vehicle. Development started in 1948, and in October of the following year a prototype was completed with a Lycoming O-290 engine. This was followed in turn by a pre-production Aerocar with an O-320 engine, used to obtain FAA Airworthiness Certification by December 1956, and four additional Aerocars for demonstration tours of the USA. By 1961 progress had been such that negotiations were under way with a major manufacturing company for quantity production.

**Model III Aerocar**

The aircraft itself comprised a four-wheel car with accommodation for two persons side-by-side, a pair of wings, and a rear fuselage section carrying the Y-configuration tail unit and drive for the pusher propeller. The flight section could be towed behind the car when required, the detachable wings having small retractable trailering wheels inset in the leading-edges. The changeover from car to aircraft was said to be possible by one person in 5 minutes. For power a Lycoming engine was fitted in the rear of the car, driving the front wheels as a road vehicle and the pusher propeller as an aircraft.

The Aerocar demonstrators were followed by the refined Model III Aerocar, with enhanced flight and road characteristics. However, to conform with then current and projected US government safety and environmental requirements for automobiles it appeared neither practicable nor economical to proceed with a production model, and the company thereafter devoted most of its activity to other aircraft (see the sixth chapter).

Arguably the strangest looking transport aircraft to enter commercial service since World War II have been the Guppies, produced in the US during the 1960s. The line started on 19 September 1962 with the first flight of the B-377PG Pregnant Guppy. This was a conversion of a Boeing Stratocruiser into a transport capable of carrying sections of large American booster rockets for NASA, initiated by Aero Spacelines. The principal modifications were the insertion of a 5.08 m (16 ft 8 in) section into the rear fuselage and the construction of a huge circular-section bubble structure over the top of the fuselage. With the new structure completed the aircraft had a maximum inside height of 6.02 m (19 ft 9 in), more than 3 m (10 ft) greater than the Stratocruiser's upper deck headroom. Regular services with the Pregnant Guppy began in July 1963, when it transported an inert Saturn S-IV stage from Los Angeles to Cape Kennedy.

An even more ambitious project followed with the construction of the larger B-377SG Super

**Aero Spacelines Super Guppy**

Guppy, designed to accommodate the third stage of a Saturn V launch vehicle and the Apollo Lunar Module adapter. Wing span and length were increased and a hinged nose section incorporated, while the new upper lobe could house cylindrical cargoes with a diameter of 7.62 m (25 ft). This version flew for the first time on 31 August 1965, powered by four 7,000 eshp Pratt & Whitney T34-P-7WA turboprop engines.

Three examples of the Guppy-201 were built, each with 4,912 eshp Allison 501-D22C turboprop engines. Two are based in Europe and have carried sections of Concorde and Airbus A300 between France and Great Britain, operated in the livery of Aéromaritime. The final two aircraft in the series were built as the B-377MG Mini Guppy, a Pratt & Whitney R-4360-B6 piston-engined version with a 6.86 m (22 ft 6 in) longer fuselage and a wider floor than the Stratocruiser, and the Allison 501-D22C-engined Guppy-101 with a hinged nose.

Of course NASA (National Aeronautics and Space Administration) itself has several research programmes currently underway, the most topical at the present time being the Space Shuttle Transportation System. The Space Shuttle is the first re-usable space vehicle, consisting basically of a booster and an Orbiter. The delta-winged Orbiter is rocket powered, the liquid propellants for these engines being carried in a large external jettisonable tank which is attached to the Orbiter at take-off. The jettisonable solid-propellant boosters are mounted either side of the large tank.

The Orbiter is launched vertically with all engines firing. At a selected altitude the boosters separate from the Orbiter and descend by parachute for recovery. Just before the Orbiter goes into orbit around the Earth it releases its propellant tank. Manoeuvres in space are performed thereafter by two smaller rocket engines in the rear of the spacecraft and by a series of small thrusters. Having performed its mission – perhaps placing satellites into orbit or scientific

**Pre-launch test-firing of engines of Orbiter OV-102** *Columbia*

# HL-10 LIFTING BODY RESEARCH VEHICLE

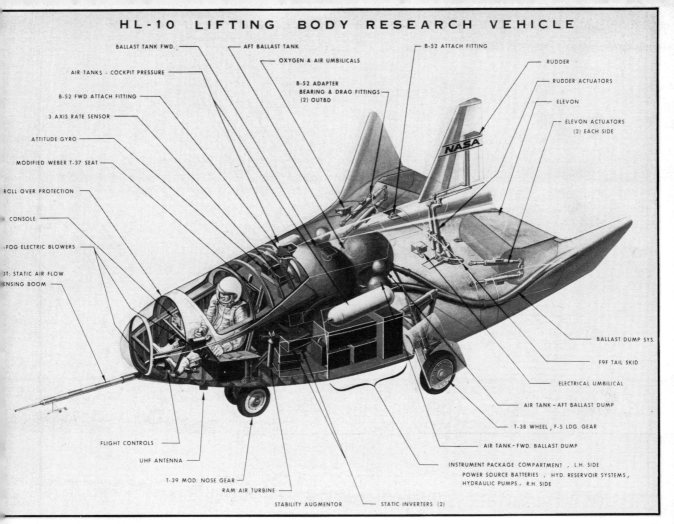

BALLAST TANK FWD.
AFT BALLAST TANK
B-52 ATTACH FITTING
OXYGEN & AIR UMBILICALS
RUDDER
AIR TANKS - COCKPIT PRESSURE
RUDDER ACTUATORS
B-52 ADAPTER BEARING & DRAG FITTINGS (2) OUTBD
B-52 FWD ATTACH FITTING
ELEVON
3 AXIS RATE SENSOR
ELEVON ACTUATORS (2) EACH SIDE
ATTITUDE GYRO
MODIFIED WEBER T-37 SEAT
ROLL OVER PROTECTION
CONSOLE
-FOG ELECTRIC BLOWERS
OT: STATIC AIR FLOW ENSING BOOM
BALLAST DUMP SYS.
F9F TAIL SKID
ELECTRICAL UMBILICAL
AIR TANK – AFT BALLAST DUMP
T-38 WHEEL , F-5 LDG. GEAR
AIR TANK – FWD. BALLAST DUMP
FLIGHT CONTROLS
UHF ANTENNA
INSTRUMENT PACKAGE COMPARTMENT , L.H. SIDE
POWER SOURCE BATTERIES , HYD. RESERVOIR SYSTEMS , HYDRAULIC PUMPS , R.H. SIDE
T-39 MOD. NOSE GEAR
RAM AIR TURBINE
STABILITY AUGMENTOR
STATIC INVERTERS (2)

**Northrop/NASA HL-10**

research – it flies back into the atmosphere and glides to its appointed landing strip.

The first Orbiter named *Enterprise* made a flight on top of a specially-prepared Boeing 747 Shuttle carrier on 18 February 1977. On 13 August a free but unpowered flight was made by the *Enterprise*, having been released from the 747 while airborne. In May 1979 it was moved to a launch complex at Kennedy Space Center, where it was used to check out ground support equipment, procedures and launch complex facilities. The second Orbiter *Columbia*, the first Space Shuttle Orbiter to be used in an Earth Orbital flight, was moved to the Space Center in March 1979 and was launched on 12 April 1981. Other Orbiters are *Challenger*, *Discovery* and *Atlantis*.

The design of the Space Shuttle Orbiter was the culmination of many years of research with lifting-body aircraft, NASA's involvement beginning in the 1960s with the M2-F1. This was a wooden wingless lifting-body glider, which was

tested successfully. Using the test results, NASA's Flight Research Center placed a contract with Northrop for two more refined metal aircraft, the first as the Northrop/NASA M2-F2 and the second as the Northrop/NASA HL-10. The M2-F2 was an Ames Research Center concept and had a basic delta planform, D-shaped in cross-section. It was controlled in pitch by a flap on the aft lower surface, and by two flaps on the upper aft surface which were used for pitch trim. These surfaces were also used for roll control. Flaps on the aft outer face of each fin were used for yaw control.

The single-seat M2-F2 was delivered to NASA in mid-1965 and, following wind tunnel testing, made an unpowered flight on 12 July 1966, having been air-launched from a Boeing B-52 Stratofortress. The flight lasted four minutes and ended with a conventional landing. After fourteen flights a 3,630 kg (8,000 lb) thrust Thiokol XLR 11 rocket engine was fitted. However two more

**Martin Marietta X-24A**

**Martin Marietta X-24B**    (*Martin Marietta*)

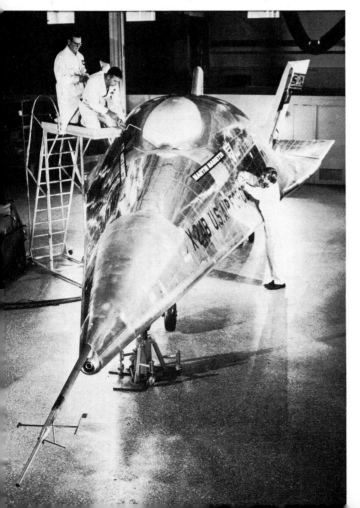

unpowered flights ended in disaster when, on 10 May 1967, the aircraft was badly damaged in a wheels-up landing. It was rebuilt as the M2-F3, supporting an additional centre fin, and performed a powered flight on 25 November 1970. Research with this aircraft continued until the end of 1972.

Meanwhile, in January 1966, the HL-10 had been delivered to NASA. Basically similar in construction to the M2-F2, it had the straight edge of its D cross-section forming the under-surface (the straight-edge of the D forming the M2-F2's upper surface). Other airframe changes included a central fin and rudder. An unpowered flight was performed on 22 December 1966 and by the end of 1971 some 37 flights had been made, 25 with power on. During the test pro-gramme it attained an altitude of 27,500 m (90,303 ft) and a speed of Mach 1.861. NASA's Flight Research Center subsequently conducted a series of tests with this aircraft to gather data on the need for the Space Shuttle to have auxiliary power for use during the landing approach. For this the Thiokol was replaced by three 227 kg (500 lb) thrust Bell hydrogen-peroxide rockets, which could be fired independently to provide the pilot with three thrust levels.

**NASA AD-1 Oblique-Wing Aircraft** (*NASA*)

Prior to the Northrop/NASA aircraft, Martin Marietta had been engaged in research along a similar line, starting in 1959. With the aim of developing a manoeuvring manned re-entry vehicle able to perform as a spacecraft in orbit, fly in the Earth's atmosphere and land conventionally, the company produced its X-23A. This small unmanned aircraft first proved the concept feasible.

In May 1966 the USAF ordered from Martin Marietta the SV-5P Pilot (Piloted Low-speed Test aircraft), which became officially designated X-24A. It was of triangular planform and 'bulbous wedge shape', with a flat bottom, rounded top and three vertical fins. Power plant was selected to be the Thiokol XLR 11, plus two Bell LLRV landing rockets (see above). It was delivered in July 1967 and during 1969 completed successfully nine unpowered flights. The first powered flight was carried out on 19 March 1970, lasting 7 minutes 15 seconds. Twenty-eight flights were performed under the powered programme, several at supersonic speeds. Maximum speed and altitude attained were Mach 1.62 and 21,765 m (71,407 ft) respectively. Eventually the X-24A was stripped down and rebuilt as the X-24B.

As the X-24B the aircraft made its first unpowered flight in August 1973. The airframe had been rebuilt with a triangular cross-section, comprising flat bottom and rounded top. Overall length had increased from 7.47 m (24 ft 6 in) to 11.43 m (37 ft 6 in), giving a very pointed appearance. Altogether this aircraft achieved six unpowered and 13 powered flights up to the spring of 1975, all rated as highly successful. Its final powered flight was made on 23 September that year, although a number of gliding flights were scheduled.

A current NASA research programme is centred on the AD-1 Oblique-Wing Aircraft, built to explore in piloted flight the viability of the pivoting wing (or oblique-wing) concept. Detail design of the AD-1 was undertaken by Mr Burt Rutan (see the sixth chapter), and the completed aircraft was delivered to NASA's Dryden Flight Research Center in March 1979. In operation it is designed to take-off, fly at low speed and land with the wing in a conventional position. For higher-speed flight the wing is pivoted at an angle of up to 60° with the fuselage, so reducing drag and possibly increasing speed and range with no increase in fuel consumption.

The single-seat AD-1 was first flown on 21 December 1979, powered by two 100 kg (220 lb) thrust Ames Industrial Corporation TRS 18-046 turbojet engines mounted on short stub wings. After eight flights with the wing in a conventional position, a flight was made in February 1980 with the wing pivoted through 5° to 15°. Testing continued, and in May that year the wing setting exceeded 45° for the first time, the aircraft's 14th flight. Test flights continue.

The final aircraft in *Fantastic Flying Machines* is the Ryan XV-8A Fleep (Flexible Wing Aerial Utility Vehicle), chosen partly because it combined features of aircraft from previous chapters – notably the Flex-Wing originated in design studies at NASA by Francis M. Rogallo – and partly because of its rightful place in a chapter devoted to shapes.

**Ryan XV-8A Fleep**

Ryan conducted much research on the Flex-Wing, under contract from the US Army, US Marine Corps and NASA. Consisting of a flexible membrane, attached to a keel and two leading-edges, the Flex-Wing offered many advantages over rigid wings and parachutes in specialised applications in manned and unmanned, powered and unpowered aircraft (drones and space vehicles).

The first piloted Flex-Wing was a simple prototype registered N140N. It was built in 1961 and was powered by a 180 hp Lycoming engine driving a pusher propeller. Prior to its construction, various types of Flex-Wing had been tested in free flight and in wind tunnels in conditions representing heights from sea level to 60,950 m (200,000 ft) and speeds up to Mach 4.9.

As a result of successful trials with N140N, Ryan received a follow-up contract from the US Army for two improved prototypes. Powered by a 210 hp Continental IO-360-A engine, the first XV-8A Fleep flew in June 1963. By July of the following year the initial flight programme had been completed.

Nowadays the Rogallo-type wing is most often seen in hang gliding circles, but many other applications have been, and are being, evaluated. Ryan investigated the idea that Flex-Wings could be folded in small packages and deployed quickly when needed as emergency wings on VTOL and STOL aeroplanes and helicopters, and, under NASA contract, it evaluated the use of a Flex-Wing to recover the first-stage Saturn space vehicle booster after burn-out. In America and South-East Asia the company evaluated a Flex-Wing Precision Drop Glider system to Army contract, designed to deliver heavy cargoes in containers released from aircraft: a similar concept was the Flex-Wing Individual Drop Glider system to enable airborne troops to land in a precise target area. For the USMC Ryan fabricated and flight tested Flex-Wing reconnaissance drones, known as Flex Bees.

One of the first aircraft mentioned in this book is the Edwards Rhomboidal of 1911, a huge bi-plane powered by a 50 hp Humber engine. It is unlikely to have ever 'hopped' or flown. The last are the NASA Oblique-Wing and the Ryan Fleep, both with unusual wings, the former successfully representing the very latest technology. The lesson is clearly definable: as long as there are men and women willing to question conventional design or methods of construction our lives will be enriched by fantastic flying machines.